Time Escapes

Joseph Esposito

ZAMIZ PRESS

RELIGION > CHRISTIANITY > POETRY
Copyright © 2018 by **Joseph Esposito**

Scripture taken from the New King James Version®. Copyright © 1982 by Thomas Nelson. Used by permission. All rights reserved.

All rights reserved. No part of this publication may be reproduced, distributed or transmitted in any form or by any means, without prior written permission.

The information in this book is not intended to replace the advice of a physician. It is for informational purposes only and any supplement, diet, exercise or spiritual program should be started under the advisement of a physician. Names, characters, places, and incidents may be a product of the author's imagination. Locales and public names are sometimes used for atmospheric purposes. Any resemblance to actual people, living or dead, or to businesses, companies, events, institutions, or locales is completely coincidental.

Author incurs sole responsibility for the content of their work and have signed an agreement that everything within the book is from their own imagination. Zamiz Press cannot be held responsible for any part of the work that resembles any other known work as it is impossible to exhaustively search for any resemblance.

Book Layout © 2017 Book Design Templates
Cover by Alexander Von Ness
Edited by R. Conrad

TIME ESCAPES/JOSEPH ESPOSITO. -- 1st ed.
ISBN 978-0-9992601-4-2

Acknowledgments

I thank everyone who challenged me, including in ways they may not have expected or intended. Each of you energized me to surpass barriers and achieve the abundant positive growth I now enjoy.

I especially thank the Almighty Father in Heaven, my Lord and Savior Jesus Christ, and the work of the Holy Spirit in my life, without whom this book would never have been written. For me, writing this book is a calling, not merely a privilege. For those who think that God does not exist, it is my deepest prayer that you reconsider. Think long and hard on your choices in this life; they have eternal consequences.

I give special thanks to my beloved wife Elisabet, who is always with me when I write and can testify to my "awakening" in 2011 in Brazil following a near-fatal bicycle accident. It was then that I first heard an inner voice tell me I could still write. The result was my first book, *Seeds of Life*.

I would also like to thank my daughter Alishia. She gave birth to my grandson Cayden, her first child, and inspired the title of *Seeds of Life*. And we welcome the arrival of our second grandchild, Addison Grace.

Finally, I thank the wonderful South American country of Brazil for all of its inspiration, amazing sights, and energy. For me, Brazil is the heart of this world.

Contents

Time Escapes 1

A Moment In Time 7

Timeout 11

Timeless 15

Twenty-Four Hours 19

Time Stealers 23

Living in the Moment 31

Time Passages 37

This Time 43

Time Exposes 47

A Matter of Time 53

Somewhere in Time 59

Time Table 63

Your Time 67

Next Time 71

In Time 75

Anytime 83

Time Works When It's Your Time 89

Time to Wake Up 97

Time After Time 103

What Time Is It? 107

Lifetime 113

Time to Imagine More Energy 121
The Power of God in Time 131

Introduction

Time escapes no one and no one escapes time. Running out of time is inevitable. With only twenty-four hours in a day, time never stops. Sleepy-minded people repeatedly pursue the futile effort to make, create and preserve time.

—

The Norwegian Escape cruise ship, Norwegian Cruise Lines' newest and largest ship to date, departed port from Miami Beach, Florida. Its destination was the Eastern Caribbean Sea. The passengers onboard, including my wife Elisabet and I, were all hoping to escape time. The early morning sun shone brightly to herald our adventure to the awaiting islands and much-anticipated sights to come.

As we pulled away from the port on the one-thousand-foot, nineteen story high cruise ship, waving like crazy along with all the other lucky passengers, those left behind on the pier were screaming senselessly and waving just as crazily. The Norwegian Escape was just three months old. It boasted a zip line and its own large water park with impossibly huge water slides. For the sport enthusiast, a giant basketball court and state of the art gym equipment beckoned, among many other amenities for the active-minded. Those with pampering in mind were spoiled by state of the art health spas, salt-water swimming pools and numerous hot tubs sprinkled throughout to relax both mind and body.

Joseph Esposito

We are all different people from different places and different backgrounds, embarking on a sparkling new vessel and a new journey into time in the sun. But there are still only twenty-four hours in a day.

World Order

As the world keeps turning, with many fires burning;
With the winds of change, a planet becoming strange;
So many sad faces;
Countries in a rage, like wild animals let out of their cage.
Very little respect, with always something to reject;
So many people unkind,
if they could only think with their mind.

Too much hate and crime;
soon it will be judgment time.
The Lord will come down to take His final walk around.
Some may be able to stay, and many will have to go away.
For some a second chance to make a stronger stance
To do what is right and stop this worldly fight.

There will be no winners amongst the sinners.
This day will come, not just for some, but for everyone.
The Lord will choose who is to win or lose.

Get ready for the moment of truth,
And hope to be able to keep your youth.
A little less playing and a lot more praying;
Our lives are getting shorter;
it is time for world order!

Joseph Esposito © 1/26/2012

Chapter 1

Time Escapes

Proverbs 1:2: To know wisdom and instruction, To perceive the words of understanding,

Claiming we don't have time because we are too busy is a common daily excuse to avoid our own denial of self-doubt that inevitably leads to failure. When something is important to us, we find the time. We make the time by not wasting time. We budget our time so that we can accomplish all of those things that are important to us.

Time escapes a little bit each moment of every day. We have a clock for a reason, to keep track of time. And to remind us to wake up each day if that is something we struggle with. Each new day is a gift from God, not to be wasted. The morning sunrise is a precious bonus, missed by many. Like a perfect cup of coffee or tea, it should be savored.

The older we become, the more swiftly time seems to pass. As a youth, it seems like we will never reach those milestones we long for. In our later years, we marvel at how quickly we not just reached, but flew past them. Now we look for ways to escape the ever-increasing passage of time; to create better strategies to capture and manage our time.

Like waking up early. As the old adage goes, "Early to bed and early to rise makes a man healthy, wealthy and wise."

Joseph Esposito

After three days at sea, everyone was anxious to get off the ship and onto dry land. Our first port of call was St. Thomas island, a tropical wonder of glorious sandy beaches and splendid tourist attractions. The locals' prosperity depended almost entirely on the tourists who flocked to the island during the busy season.

Amidst unspeakably beautiful weather and friendly hosts, we traveled to Megan's Bay. Iguanas lurked in the trees and small sea turtles swam about in the crystal-clear water. We blissfully lazed around in all of the tranquility as the day slipped away and time escaped.

The next day we arrived on the island of Tortola. Tortola's beauty is marked by its high mountain terrain and the stunning cliffs overlooking its postcard Caribbean beaches. Treacherous roads led us past spectacular view after spectacular view before we reached the beaches on the other side of the island. The trip itself, in a passenger trolley-like bus, followed twisting curves all the way up, while dodging cars going in the opposite direction on the other side of the road, was quite an adventure. The locals might be accustomed to this, but it was definitely not what we typically experienced on a daily basis back home on our Connecticut roads!

With barely three hours to spare before our giant ship left port, we made it back to the beach in Tortola. The sun was scorching hot and the beach was packed with people and vendors. One man with a wheelbarrow pushed coconuts with a bottle of rum. Something for everyone. We simply wanted a cool place to sit and relax for a couple of hours. We spied a young girl hurrying over to some tourist looking for a lounge chair with an umbrella. "Fifteen dollars," she quickly blurted. Time is money: on the ship, off the ship, on the beach, and off the beach. Everywhere. Taxi busses waited to take people to their destinations. For many, like us, that included the cruise ships tied up at the local piers.

After we departed Tortola we spent a day steaming at sea. We were scheduled to make our final port call at Nassau Bahamas. However, someone had to be helicoptered off the ship at three that morning. The unscheduled detour and delay caused us to miss our final port call. Instead we steamed back to Miami. It seemed both fitting and ironic that when I started this cruise and this book, I chose the title "Time Escapes." With one unexpected event, our final scheduled port call was gone. The time we planned there lost.

It is easy to think that life is not fair. We lost something that we paid for; planned on. As did every other passenger on the ship. What about the person who had to be taken off and his or her family? Was he or she okay? And what might have happened in Nassau Bahamas that did not because we did not go there? Was it God's plan that we, or someone else, not go? Was a tragedy somehow avoided for someone, or for all of us?

We all have plans for our lives, but they are not always God's plans. When things do not go as we think they should, we need to change our point of view. Everything happens for a reason.

With twenty-four hours each day, if we will allow God's light to guide us there is nothing in this life that is not attainable. There is no "change order" in our plans that can throw us off stride, because we will see it for what it is: redirection by the One who leads us on the path He wants us to take.

Elisabet and I arrived in Brazil on December 30, 2017, for a ten-week visit. Because of the time difference it took about a week to fully adjust. This was my tenth time in Brazil and I stayed at my mother-in-law's home. It is always a blessing to be able to spend time there with loved ones.

I find that I use my time there so much differently than I do at home. I am out of my comfort zone, but the change is good for me. Each time I go there, I learn to be a better person. I learn to see and hear things differently. I use my time much differently in Brazil than I do back home.

I pray.

The first time I went to Brazil was 1996, one year after I married Elisabet. The second time was in 1998, then 2004, 2008, 2010 and 2011 when I had a terrible bicycle accident early in the morning. A wild Pitbull caused me to crash into a cement post about four feet tall. The pain was horrific and ultimately resulted in my first book, the "Seeds of Life." My daughter married, and my grandson Cayden Joseph was born in 2012. His birth inspired the title of the book.

Two thousand twelve began with pain, and a lot of it. I was able to capitalize on it by seeking God through prayer. But I had a long way to go. In 2013 we returned to Brazil. I was still abusing my body with alcohol. Despite that, I continued my pursuit of the martial arts at Academia Tokyo. I first began this pursuit in 2010, when I met Instructor Geraldo, the owner of the school.

My demons were powerful back then, however, and every time I returned home I returned to old ways and habits, which included abusing myself and my time. I was unable to own the change I so desperately wanted and needed until 2015. Since then, I have not had a drop of alcohol. In 2016 we returned to Brazil and I earned my brown belt in Shotokan, the Japanese martial art that I love and respect so dearly.

In 2018, once again I found myself sober and ready for the greatest chapter in my life to be written. Once again, I found the inspiration to write a book – this book. I pray that you will also find it inspirational and uplifting.

Time may seem like a mere four-letter word, but it is essential to understand its meaning for your life. Most people waste far too much of their time in one way or another, especially in this modern age.

If you could return to yesterday, what would you like to have back to do differently? Finding what was once lost and feeling good about it and yourself can be a reminder and a game changer in more ways than one.

Time is not going to wait for you and it may take the rest of your life to catch up and find what you are truly looking for. Don't be a victim of your circumstances.

Change your inner clock and time will not matter anymore because you will be flowing in the moment of the now. Try not to look to far into your future. Goals are great to have and to achieve those goals is even greater.

Going full speed ahead can be an accident waiting to happen when our focus is distracted.

Time will not wait for us. It may take the rest of our life to catch up and find what we are looking for. Do not be a victim of circumstances that you create because you are reckless with your time.

Being in control and staying in control are completely different. To stay in control, one must have and keep a selfish schedule, constantly, without interruption.

When we lose control, we lose time.

Chapter 2

A Moment In Time

Proverbs 1:3: To receive the instruction of wisdom, Justice, judgment, and equity;

Taking a moment to reflect on bad behavior, or a conversation going in the wrong direction, provides insight for the next battle within oneself. Thoughts can become challenging when the signal to self is weak.

Moments are increments of time that travel at the speed of light. If one cannot capture the moment, it evaporates and disappears forever. Staying in the moment is a process of elimination. Staying in the moment, while being in the moment, is impossible. Time does not stop during the moment.

Journaling enables one to save time and capture the inner self. Others may only know who we portray on the outside. They will know the person we let them see, happy or sad, nice or not, but not our real self. If we know and are comfortable with who we are, then we will not hide behind a false front and others will also see our true selves.

I consider myself to be a messenger of positivity. However, I have thrown up road blocks in my own way for years. I have written three books, but only published two. I have not reached out publicly. I allowed that to become a stumbling block in my life. With my latest trip to Brazil, I finally removed this block.

Joseph Esposito

I have tried and failed many times to conquer the demons that scream in my head. They play a game of give and take and plant false insecurities within me that have no existence at all except within this crazy game that I permit to take place. It really is all in my mind. Everything I ever wanted to have or wished to become is always within my reach. I just need to stay the path God has planned and wait for His timing.

Waiting is often not a pleasurable experience, but it does grow character. Sometimes the wait is more valuable than the prize that awaits. The wait can be a journey of growth. So often when we get something we want, we forget about the waiting process and what we learned or discovered while waiting. We are on to the next "thing" that we want, and quickly resent the next wait we have to endure.

If we do not learn to appreciate the wait, we start to feel put upon, irritated, sorry-for-ourselves, angry. These negative feelings do not improve the situation. They only build up, accumulate, and foster bitterness and negativity. Satan loves to work with these feelings to break a person down and convince them they are not worthy of anything good.

After fifty-eight years, I have learned God's ways and believe that I am supposed to write about my experiences and share them with the world.

God, the unseen Creator of the universe, holds all the power between Him and His son, Jesus Christ. His Word, the Bible, is a wondrous book of mysteries and truths that have happened or are going to happen. It is a book of the past and the future of the world. Written over two thousand years ago, the Bible is not a book that is understood in a moment of time.

We see only what we want to see. In so doing, we may completely miss the richness of what we do not, or cannot, see. Where does the wind come from? How does the sun shine so brightly? Why do the seasons change? Where does time go?

In a moment our life can change, whether from a tragic accident or a providential event like buying a winning lottery ticket. Though it may seem obvious that one of these will have a positive impact and the other a negative impact on our life, in truth either can have a positive or negative impact, depending on events that follow.

What is important is how we are changed by events that occur in our lives. We can change only when we are ready. There are so many forces that shape us: our genetics; experiences; family; friends; beliefs; disappointments; likes; dislikes; talents; opportunities and those we missed; teachers; people who hurt us; essentially everything. We process and assimilate all of these experiences into our character. There are opportunities all along the way for trouble or triumph.

If we knew where we were going from the start, we could probably find a way to get there much faster and save ourselves a lot of struggle and strife along the way. Being uncomfortable is the new comfort zone for many of us humans today. His is a direction that leads to an unknown destiny He has planned for us. If we will let Him lead, we are all we need to get there. Stop procrastinating and jump into life. If you can walk and talk, then you should be running and speaking loud and clear, in the direction of the masses that need to hear your message.

Time is priceless, but the cost of losing it by not using it can become high. Years wasted because of a bad relationship, or a terrible childhood, can play over and over again if we allow them to. Wake yourself up, literally. Earlier and earlier each day if necessary. Create that space in time for yourself. As the seasons change, become the change that is right for you to gain momentum in a positive direction to another level in time.

Chapter Three

Timeout

Proverbs 1:6: To understand a proverb and an enigma, The words of the wise and their riddles.

Many people sleep so much more than they really need, then complain about not having enough time. Doing what needs to be done always starts with time. Being on time is essential to creating great habits.

A healthy lifestyle helps lead to longevity. As with so many people, I have not always led a healthy lifestyle. Addictions and substance abuse are time stealers at best; at worst they can ruin or steal our youth and even our life.

Knowing the difference between right and wrong timing can take a lifetime to learn, when one only wakes up to have another pity party.

Staying up all night partying as I have so many times because of a victory of self-achievement is understandable. But when staying up all night because of a bad addictive habit can steal not only your youth, but your time as well.

Staying sober and learning normal behavior may not seem normal at all. In fact, because of substance abuse and bad addictions time stealers can ruin your normal life as you had once known.

It is not too late to learn to live again. Starting anything over is almost always a difficult process and painful experience. But the cost of not doing it is too high to contemplate. Ask any family member of a chronic addict. Giving up and giving in is just the first step of several in the process of getting well before becoming hopelessly lost in a reckless and dangerous lifestyle.

Hope equals action. Taking control over our actions will allow us to have new hope. Staying in control will allow us to thrive on a hunger to become something more than we were before our sobriety. Saving ourselves to a state of redemption will allow us a new freedom that we never knew existed.

Gaining momentum in a positive direction will allow us to lead and not follow. Tell yourself that change is the new normal, and for a good reason. Because life depends on it. We owe it to ourselves and to all the people we ever cared about to change course and reconsider how we spend our time.

Being able to trust ourselves alone will be a whole new game changer. Once we escape our time-stealers, we will start to become trustworthy to ourselves and others.

It is important to take a vacation from ourselves to escape time in a positive place. Go on vacation to "level-up" and open your eyes to see the sights that surround you – maybe for the first time in a very long time.

How much time have we missed? How many times have we gone somewhere and not only disappointed ourselves, but the other person or people we were with? Be honest about this. It is forgivable to occasionally act stupid when drunk or highly medicated. But to repeatedly abuse everyone around us is just not fair and not excusable.

When a mishap or an accident takes place and disrupts our time, we realize how much time really means to us. A wake-up call to attract our attention. A message that we need to shift direction and rethink our life's situations and time-out.

Our life may have spun out of control. If we can, we must revive ourselves and realize that this life is only temporary. We must choose a path of righteousness and move forward past the negativity that has been holding us back. It is only too late if we do not wake up to the light of God while we still have breath in our body.

Nothing is permanent in this life. Until we realize that and find the fire inside that will allow us to change, we will not see the light God is shining in our direction. If we let Him, He will lift our spirit and energize us into infinity and redemption. Through Him, we will find a whole new person that we never knew existed.

Chapter Four

Timeless

Proverbs 3:5: Trust in the LORD with all your heart, and lean not on your own understanding;

It is impossible to stay timeless. Even with make-up and plastic surgery, one will still have inner parts that are aging and breaking down. Despite the best vitamins, supplements and exercise, we are still going to grow old. Even prayer will not save us from old age and death.

Keeping a clear head will probably be your biggest challenge, with all the noise pollution and corruptive mindsets that want to control everything all the time.

Take care of your mind and your body will follow your thought pattern. No, it will not be easy unless you have been doing this since you were born. Most of us learn from our past mistakes by losing our time, because of that negative mindset that everyone has.

To say that you do not have a negative side would be a lie that you tell yourself. For example,

(1) Do you ever get upset with yourself or another person because something has not gone as planned?

(2) Do you feel positive when you have an injury or an accident?

(3) When you lose something like a job or a loved one, does that make you happy or sad?

Let's face it and be real about negative and positive thoughts. It's okay to get angry, and quite frankly it is completely normal, unless you are a robot that has no real feelings.

Anyone who claims to never have a negative thought is lying to themselves. No one can be positive all the time. But we do not have to be negative all the time either. That is a choice.

We will have negative thoughts and feelings. We cannot escape that fact. We need to recognize them and own them. I have anger issues that I continue to work on. I often, in anger or irritation, fail to keep my mouth shut when I should, and I say the wrong thing. I usually slip-up and say all the wrong things and then feel real stupid because of it.

The key is not to dwell on negative things. The key is not to dwell on the negative. It's okay to get pissed-off and then take a deep breath and think of something that always makes you smile and move on from there.

Learning is a lifelong process of give and take. If we are only taking and not giving, then we will have a serious problem eventually. When we see a blue sky or the fruits of a beautiful garden that we planted years ago, we see the handiwork of the Creator God and can begin to sense His timeless quality.

Music and art, even if written or created hundreds of years ago, can still hold the same power today as when first written or created. People in some cultures do not seem to age in the same way as other cultures. Their skin does not wrinkle; their hair does not thin or fall out; they do not become overweight or arthritic. The martial arts, as well, have a timeless quality, beauty and appeal.

Getting dressed up for a date, or a party, we always like to look good. For me, with very little hair left, it is okay to not have a full head of hair. It is not my fault that my hairline has receded.

Part of our growth will portray a new character over time. We will just have to adjust accordingly and not worry about what others are thinking. Some may never have that problem and get to keep their wrinkleless face and full head of hair. Depending on where you are from in the world, has a lot to do with our health too.

In Asia, the people seem to be ageless. No wrinkles, no fat, and always smiling. Why is that?

They might experience less stress because most of the people that live in those countries know the martial arts and eat differently than the rest of the world. Every martial artist that I know, is very happy and that is how I want to become, as I continue my journey to black belt level in two different styles.

Our time is our own unless we are a prisoner in jail or a prisoner of our own devices. Nothing created by man lasts forever. In this modern world, we travel a disconnected path because of electronic devices of all sorts that keep us connected to one another and the Internet, but largely disconnected from our Creator. Times are changing every day – sometimes every hour or minute or second – whether we want change or not.

I dream often when I am in Brazil. One was about the Feds coming onto a construction site with badges and walkie-talkies to get information in an attempt to crack down on illegal immigrants and builders violating the laws.

God's laws are timeless, but governments have their own laws. Man-made laws. In my view, corruption runs deep in Washington and so many other places and it is being exposed every day. Only the honest people in this world will survive and the liars and cheaters will be punished and prosecuted. The government is a group of greedy, selfish people. They are always on the take and are in the process of eliminating themselves. The irony is they do not even realize it.

As they say, money is the root of all evil, and it could not be more truthful today. A timeless matter of stealing other people's gains for their own benefit and not ours.

Chapter Five

Twenty-Four Hours

*P*roverbs 1:11: If they say, "Come with us; let us lie in wait to shed blood, let us lurk secretly for the innocent without cause;

Everyone has one thing in common, we all have twenty-four hours to start each day. I have now read the Bible four times; I do not find "twenty-four" written anywhere in the Book of Life. The numbers seven and twelve are used often. God created the earth in six days and rested on the seventh. Seven is sacred. The seventh day is a day of rest. It is the Sabbath day. It is a holy number. Twelve is also holy. There were twelve tribes of Israel. Jesus had twelve apostles.

Twenty-four hours may not seem like a lot of time. In reality, it is more than enough if we can figure out how to stop wasting time and gain more by doing more. Stop looking at the clock. Clocks are everywhere. Most people go to work by the clock, take breaks by the clock, and leave work by the clock. People measure their commute time by the clock.

I am fortunate that I am self-employed most of the time, though I also sub-contract to another source. I have never enjoyed punching a clock or having my breaks scheduled at a particular time. I eat when I am hungry, not when the clock tells me I am supposed to eat.

I believe that is why I am able to write. Though I have only ten years of formal schooling, writing is my escape into a world of truth. I write from my heart. I have spoken already of my first book, "Seeds of Life." My second book is "On a Mission of Nutrition." This is my third book.

God is my influence. He has shown me the way because of my never-ending belief in Him and through my childhood pain. My parents divorced when I was very young. Their separation was very difficult on me emotionally. I found school difficult after that and I used it as an excuse to rebel and find trouble everywhere I went. With God's help I do not cause trouble anymore and I have set aside my bad habits.

It has been a long journey to find myself. It all began when I stopped drinking. I picked up the Bible and started to study God's Word and pray daily. The Holy Bible is the book of truth. Everything you need is there. It will never lead you in the wrong direction. It will never lie to you.

There is nothing worse than bad love. It kills the spirit, breaks the heart and confuses the mind. If one wants to go on a rollercoaster ride, visit the carnival. Do not allow a bad relationship to kill you slowly and take away your hopes and dreams of what love can and should be.

Being and living in the moment is the only way we can succeed at anything. If our heart or mind is in the wrong place, our spirit will be lost. Physical beauty is only skin deep.

This is my first book that is all me, not divinely-inspired. This is my time of change and growth and I am on a journey that I hope to take the reader on as well, believer or non-believer. If you are someone who has difficulty getting out of your own way, as I have been.

My twenty-four hours are now journaled and lived with a passion of self-love with God in front of and all around me. It is my goal to find my truth and reveal it through this book. Our time is our own, but it is God who ultimately controls and allows us to use our time for His advantage and not our own.

I say this because when we continually make the same mistakes over and over again, we start to struggle and doubt. We get stuck and our momentum stalls. We start to blame others for our own faults. We have just gotten in our own way again.

If we do not believe in our Creator and cede control of our life to Him, we may find ourselves going to Hell right here on earth. Maybe you have already been there. Only He can give us a greater purpose for our life. Through Him we will find power and an inner strength that we never knew we possessed. God has no limits. The only limits we have are the ones we place on ourselves. But He is the key to becoming limitless.

We are surrounded by an unseen power and an unseen world. We are being watched and listened to – sure by the cameras and electronic devices of this intrusive physical world – but also by the supernatural world that surrounds us. The armies of Satan and of Heaven are real. The light of Jesus Christ shines upon us. It allows us to see our past mistakes, but it also shows us the way forward, in forgiveness and grace, redeemed to become what we were created to be.

Dreams can come true if we are persistent and refuse to listen to the voice that holds self-doubt. We prevent ourselves from rising when we talk ourselves out of something because of money or fear. Let go. Let God. If we reach out, He will find us and make our dreams come true.

Like a driver on a racetrack, relentless with his skill, moving faster and faster to maneuver around the other drivers to win, only a select few become winners. If a driver is not careful, or if there is a problem with the car, or if he is just unlucky that particular day, an accident will occur. He could be badly injured, or even die.

Like the driver, we can learn to control the power we have, but we cannot control every variable. Giving away our heart for a foolish fling can destroy a lifetime of joy in just twenty-four hours. Staying true to ourselves is hard; staying true to others challenging at best. We all make mistakes. It is the process by which we learn. Only Jesus

Joseph Esposito

Christ lived a perfect life. For the rest of us, it will take every ounce of energy and extreme dedication to even come close to perfection some of the time, let alone all of the time. Just trying is exhausting.

Our generation has come a long way from where we started, many years ago. Our children and grandchildren should be able to excel during their lifetimes. It is up to us to see that they are brought up well, cared for, and given every opportunity to be greater than us.

Chapter Six

Time Stealers

*P*roverbs 1:10: My son, if sinners entice you, Do not consent.

Time stealers are all around us. They are in bars and clubs and many other places that allow us to relax our minds. Going to a bar is not the end of the world, just do not allow yourself to live there. Know your limits. Getting drunk will steal away a lot of time and will shorten your life.

If we never start drinking, we will never have a drinking problem. It is better to be sober.

The only true way to know is by experimenting. It typically happens on a special occasion, like a holiday, or birthday, or some other celebration. Maybe you just hit the legal age for drinking. You have that first drink, which usually turns into more than one. A person either falls in love with alcohol or gets horribly sick the first time and does not want to experience that feeling again.

I drank alcohol for about forty years. It was only three years ago when I knew I had enough of my time taken away from me.

Drugs are not much better, including those that one's doctor prescribes. Addiction is all too common. If one is not careful, one can slip into darkness for a very long time. Many years can pass before one hits that proverbial "bottom." It can come in any number of ways, most of them pretty much devastating and avoidable but for the addiction.

It is okay to medicate from an injury or surgery, but do not fool yourself that you are smarter or stronger than the drug your doctor prescribes. Addiction creeps up like a sly fox and then grips tighter than a python. When starting any medication with an addictive quality, understand its properties and have a tapering plan in place before you start and someone to hold you accountable.

Losing control is another time stealer. As infants, we learn to cry to get our needs met. As toddlers, we perfect this and take it to the next level, learning to manipulate adults to get what we want and to punish them when we do not with temper tantrums. I still have an anger issue that I work on daily, because I take just about everything personally. But bad behavior only prolongs the agony of not having what we want when we want it.

Time stealers are manipulative stumbling blocks that are in plain sight; all we need to do is pick them up and use them. Habits out-of-control will only hurt us and everyone around us. But the one we hurt the most will be our self. Do not sell yourself to a drug or a bad habit of sorts. There are so many great things to look forward to, with the element of surprise always just around the corner.

Are you the boss? It is great to be in charge and have people work for you. Unfortunately, that is also a good way to slip up. We start to think that we can take a long lunch, leave early, or take the day off. Then a few drinks, drugs, an affair, or something else enters into the picture. Before we know it, a bad habit has formed. If we think no one knows, we are fooling ourselves. I know. I have been there, done that. It did not work before; it will not work now. I do not care how well you handle your drugs, your alcohol binges, or whatever your pleasure, you are moving in the wrong direction and time will not be on your side.

This is one reason I am writing this book. I did it and I survived to tell my story. Maybe you will too, but maybe you won't be so lucky my friend. We are only allowed so much time. If we knew how much time we really had, we probably would not waste so much of it.

Have you ever gone on a vacation and lost a couple of days, or more, from being sick? On the last day you realize that your surroundings are incredible, but unfortunately your time is up, and it is time to return home again.

My tenth time in Brazil on vacation, I looked back on the first eight. I drank a lot and had friends over who brought wine or some other alcoholic beverage. The day and/or night would pass in an alcohol haze. I would wake up the next day and vow never to do that again. Of course, I would. The parties were great. They were also great time stealers.

Now when I am in Brazil I am sober. I feel better. My time is not lost or stolen.

I used to think I needed a couple of drinks to talk to a girl because I am shy at first. I did not know better. Because of that, it has taken me more than half of my life to realize I had a problem. I was never a social drinker. I never thought I had a problem because I was not an alcoholic. I did not drink all the time. But when I did drink, I could not stop myself, even when the bar closed. I made sure there was alcohol at home, or something else, or both.

It is important that I am honest as I write about this lifestyle. Had I not wasted so much time in those earlier years, I would probably be a great martial artist by now. But my priorities and my focus were off. I messed up. When I was twenty years old, with my life ahead of me, I quit the school I was in and moved to Florida to live with my Mom. I mistakenly thought that if I left my drug-addicted friends behind I would also leave my problems behind.

South Florida, I found out the hard way, was a mecca of drugs and alcohol. After hours clubs were everywhere. When the regular bars closed at two a.m., the bottle clubs opened. Talk about going straight to hell. Between the topless and bottomless bars, where the dancers practically live (another huge time stealer, not to mention costly habit), I was well on the way to completely poisoning my body, heart, mind and soul.

The only good thing that came out of Florida for me was the birth of my daughter Alishia. She woke me up enough to realize that I might have a greater purpose to live for.

But I was still arrogant. I thought I knew what I was doing because I had people working for me. I still had money in my pocket and I worked every day. I must be respectable. That was just another lie I told myself every twenty-four hours.

I know I am truly blessed, because I should have died many times over. Believe me, it is only too late when you actually take your last breath. Until then, we can decide to change. There is still time. Between the time and money wasted, the years wallowing through my numerous pity parties, and knowing now that what I thought of as living was really a form of death, I find myself surprised that God has any use for me at all. But that is why He is God.

Now my daughter is twenty-nine years old and I have a beautiful grandson who looks up to me. He has no notion of the person I once was. I would like to keep it that way. I cannot protect him from the world – I know that. But the less negativity he knows, the better. I do not want to plant the wrong seeds in his innocent little mind.

When someone kicks your behind because they found you drunk or polluted on some other substance, try thanking them instead of cursing them. I never did. I was always rebellious. I had all the answers. I knew exactly what I was doing. Except that I did not. My demons had control and I failed to appreciate that the person kicking me was desperately trying to shake them loose and set me free.

We will never have all of the answers to our problems. I cannot give them to you here. I do not have them. There are more problems than solutions. The sooner we know that, the better we will use our time. Not everything has to be solved or fixed. We will come out on the other side. We will be okay. Without alcohol or drugs to help us get there.

When I was twenty years old, I would get drunk and think I was the strongest person in the bar. I would then show off my karate kicks and sometimes end up in a fight as a result. Fortunately, I was always able to walk away without serious injury. But I was stupid.

I have two older brothers who enjoyed inflicting pain on me, especially when they drank. They were another reason why I left home. Time stealers come in all shapes and sizes.

Once we pick our poison and fall completely in love with it, only time will reveal if and when we will finally be able to walk away from it, and with how many scars. I was able to do it on my own, but for many an intervention and professional help are required. Sometimes multiple attempts are needed. Do not give up. Do not forget about the scars. They must be addressed.

God has thrice blessed me: my daughter; my grandson; and my wife of twenty-two years. My wife has suffered with and because of me more than anyone and she is still with me. For what reason, I still do not know. She is a brave, strong woman. I once said that if God sent me a sober woman I would quit everything. I lied. I should be severely punished for waiting so many years to make good on my promise to Him.

Please do not think you can never change. If I can change, so can you. Time may not be on my side anymore. I may have run out of chances to get it right. But I can honestly and whole heartedly tell you this much: my grandson means more to me than life itself; and there is nothing I would not do for him to keep him going in the right direction.

I call Cayden my "light in shining armor." At only five years old, he already has one year of martial arts under his belt and he is an above average student in school. The love his mother provides is unconditional. He is so much fun to be with. When I look at him, I see the splendor and promise of God.

Maybe that is why I get the chance to do it right this time. I fell short when raising my daughter. I was a single parent for the first seven years of her life. I was never a bad father, but I was not a good one either. I lost a lot of quality time with her because I did not deal with my own demons. She paid the price for that, even after I married. I know life now, because I live it.

Alcohol abuse runs in my bloodline. I realize that is an excuse, but it is also a true statement. My father, at eighty-seven, is still drinking. My brothers both drink. My grandparents drank. All to excess.

I finally quit because I chose love. I chose life. I chose my grandson over myself.

I struggle in martial arts these days. I am not a young man anymore and keeping up with younger, stronger, more agile people will never be an easy task. If I knew then, when I was young as they are now, what I know now about how the choices I made would play out, I might be an unstoppable force today.

Now, I happily let my grandson steal my time. I cannot give him enough of my time. What a joy to watch him grow and learn.

When I was young, I did not have the opportunities he has today. Martial arts came to America through people like Bruce Lee – a true master – and Chuck Norris. Only a few fortunate students had the opportunity to train here in the early days. When Bruce Lee died, a bright light was extinguished forever. A handful of his students had to pick up the pieces and continue his legacy of teaching new students. These days, martial arts schools are everywhere. My grandson has a great instructor, very much like mine in Brazil.

It is important to keep our mind occupied and focused on growth, no matter our age. Doing so will help us keep our heart open. We will not learn the most valuable life lessons sitting on a bar stool with a drink in front of us, or watching a beautiful girl take her clothes off while dancing in front of us. These are time stealers.

I have found complete fulfillment by reading and studying the Bible. The Word of God is rich and true. The answers to all of life's questions and troubles are found within its pages. It may be old, but it is timeless in its wisdom. God will never steer you wrong. My personal training in the martial arts is also physically and mentally fulfilling and challenging. I strongly recommend both if you are searching. What do you have to lose? You may be surprised by what you gain.

Get your time back. Stop doing whatever it is that is holding you back. Change course and become the greatest version of yourself.

Chapter Summary

Time stealers:
- Not going to sleep on time
- Waking up too late
- Living in the past; not allowing your thoughts to change
- Hanging out with the wrong crowd
- Not managing your time in a positive manner
- Not believing in higher power
- Not making room for change
- Listening to negativity
- Eating toxic, processed food
- Not loving or caring about yourself

Time Savers:
- Going to bed early
- Waking up very early
- Staying strong and healthy
- Reading scriptures
- Stop lying to yourself
- Remove self-doubt
- Control your conversations
- Creating a better character
- Speaking only the truth
- Show more love to others

Chapter Seven

LIVING IN THE MOMENT

*P*roverbs 2:21: For the upright will dwell in the land, And the blameless will remain in it;

Living in the moment is not an easy task, unless we have always done it from our childhood. Moments come and go all day and all night. Capturing the moment, like taking a picture, is essential to remind us that our lives are filled with beauty. Filling our minds with positive images is a great way to secure a positive mindset.

Our minds are similar to a bank account. What we put in our memory bank and keep there is what we accumulate to become mentally and spiritually rich or poor. We all like to have a healthy bank account to secure our future. When we do not have much money, we tend to feel nervous and maybe even a bit desperate. We can forget our true value. We might make hasty choices and work for less money than we are worth, or even steal.

To quote old sayings, "sometimes we may have to eat crow," or "a half a loaf is better than no loaf at all." I do not like crows. They are scavengers. I know they are God's creatures, but their real function is to consume dead carcasses and other spoilage.

Moments and habits go hand in hand. Negative or positive, moments can turn into days and nights of endless possibilities. Living and planning these moments – molding them into the perfect schedule – can become a frustrating challenge.

There are no days off from oneself. We can choose to love ourselves or hate who we have become. It is inevitable that we will all get lost occasionally as we navigate through life. We can stay lost or dig deep and find our purpose to help us get back on track.

Learning is a lifelong process of taking wrong turns and making course corrections to get back on track. As we mature, one of two things will happen: we will lose focus and drift further away from our goals or we will sharpen our focus and commit to a course that leads to our becoming a better person.

It will never hurt anybody to read the Bible. We just might be surprised at the treasure, and the answers, we will find within the pages. One of God's promises is to look and we will find; knock and the door will be opened; ask and you will get what you ask for (Matthew 7:7.) God is real and lives inside of us if we will only invite Him in. He wants to show us the greater purpose He has for us. He wants to let His light shine through us into the darkness.

Take a moment to visualize where you are and where you would like to be. Hard work may not be pleasurable, as the saying goes, "No pain, no gain." Changing a negative into a positive may only take a moment, but we must first think it into being before we can act on it.

Change takes time. Some change takes a little bit of time; some takes more. When backed up by twenty-four hours in a day, and a well-planned use of time, we will see results. Living in the moment is just that. Nothing more; nothing less. We would all like to have instant gratification every time, but the universe does not work that way. Some things are not meant to happen too fast.

Step-by-step. Day-by-day. Following God's plan is the only way to build true momentum between us and God.

God created us all equal. He gives us His love. Man destroys love, and many other things along the way. We are not born bad, but we can become spoiled. A rotten seed can take root and grow within us.

It can corrupt our mind and heart. We learn to hold onto hate. We learn to bear grudges. We learn prejudice. We become combative with others because we believe we are right and they are wrong. We forget how to empathize and compromise. We forget how to love.

Two wrongs never make a right. This should be a good enough reason to look the other way. It should be a good enough reason to keep silent when we want to argue or criticize or lash out. Reflect on the day past.

Living within the moment, utilizing our time, requires us to sacrifice some things that are comfortable, noise pollution and distractions that are time stealers. They are everywhere. Learn to appreciate different things. Let your mind and senses absorb the wonders of creation. The things that most people do not see. The things that speak of God. Be in the moment.

Do not get too far ahead of yourself with the busyness of what the world offers. We can find ourselves moving in a hundred different directions at once. It is enough to make our heads hurt. Slow down. Enjoy the ride. Appreciate the moment. We are about to reach that fork in the road.

For me, because of my stubbornness, I chose the Bible and everything inside of it, to show me a new way to live in the moment and here I am early-rising and writing about everything that is told to me.

To launch myself and all my works, I may have to pay someone to kick that door open, so I can speak my works and save some lives.

We are all saviors of different types the only problem is we may think that we are not able to help anyone because we may not be strong enough to help ourselves.

Living in the moment, depending on where you are, has everything to do with how you react to your surroundings.

If you are sitting in a jail cell or a hospital bed, obviously, it will not be pretty. However, it can be very rewarding, once you move past the pain of being locked up or tied down to a bed.

God's teachings are nothing less than relentless. If you have something that you are supposed to be doing, you will be guided to that purpose, just as I am being directed once again.

Once you start believing that a shift has come, you can pass-up the old you. Put fire to the flame and burn all your pain and go from losing to winning. That is when you have arrived.

Being up-front and getting personal may not be easy for some. Until you do that, giving away all your inner demons on a stage and representing yourself like you never have before, is when your light will shine through.

Too many people are stuck on money and forget their true value.

To have a million dollar bill may be a great thing. I listen to the song from Whitney Houston called <u>Million Dollar Bill</u> and realize that unfortunately it did not help her. Her money killed her.

It's very sad to lose such a bright light, such as she was, a woman that found fame and fortune at a very young age. She traveled the world, singing to everyone with that amazing voice and beautiful smile. But, her demons were very strong. She had stardom two times, yet still allowed her demons to overpower her.

I miss her as if I knew her personally. She was my all-time favorite singer and one I never got to see live on stage.

Another great was Michael Jackson. He is a perfect example. He had a genius mindset and became super-rich at a very young age. He too had demons haunting him. I think that because of his endless energy he was not able to sleep well. I think his death could have been avoided if his doctor did his job, instead of letting Michael die.

Michael's had a song called the <u>Man in the Mirror</u> that he wrote about change within himself, but again his demons were so much stronger.

Living with getting high, getting drunk, having too much fun because you are obsessed by spending money, will dig your grave much faster. All that light that you had will only put you into and leave you in a very dark place.

You see so many of the songwriters and singers with fame and fortune. We think that they have it made, because of their wealth. The problem is that the only time they are truly happy is when they are on-stage and to be on-stage they must keep working for that next new song.

God had given them a greater purpose than most will never get to have, the only problem is that they could not enjoy living in the moment.

Chapter Eight

TIME PASSAGES

Proverbs 1:5: A wise man will hear and increase learning, And a man of understanding will attain wise counsel,

Staying in Brazil was a huge time passage for me to allow my mind to change direction and reflect on my life. I never imagined that I would make one trip to this country, let alone ten.

God is working on something and wants to use me as a messenger. I accept His offer and will do my best to get the word out that, as time passes, He is choosing a select few who are willing and able to do His work, regardless of where they are.

While in Brazil I took a welcome break from American television. The channels there are different and it allowed me to change the channel in my head and tune in more closely to God. When the New Testament portion of the Bible was being lived, Jesus was the teacher to many of those who would write the various chapters and take His gospel to the world. How amazing it would have been to walk with Him and sit with Him, hearing His words from His own mouth.

I never really knew who I was before I wrote my first book. It was a journey of self-discovery. I wrote it while I was in Brazil. I write in places and at times when I am inspired. Brazil is one of those places. Another book was written when Elisabet and I were on our Caribbean cruise. There was a fire inside of me and the book poured out in four short days. I could not have prevented it and it would have been a sin to try. Inspiration comes, sometimes when you least expect it.

I know I claimed earlier that this book was my own work, but I could not keep God's inspiration out of it. Initially I thought it was true that this was my own work. It is not. You get what you need, even when you are not looking for it, when you do the work of the Almighty. God's work is finished, even before it starts. God only needs to find the messenger that is willing to do the work.

I hope this time I can get this book in the right hands and send it around the world where it needs most to be read. I have to trust that God will place it where he wants His light to shine and bring His positive message and Godly spirit to those who need it most, as I did. Trying to communicate a message from a higher power and find the intended audience can be a daunting task.

I have come to know that I am never alone, even when I am by myself. My heart feels His presence at all times, watching and guiding me no matter where I am. Writing is therapeutic for me. It is surprising to find myself enjoying something that I never learned in school. The process itself is healing, largely because it is God-inspired.

When Jesus returns from his own time passage – in the Second Coming – people will realize too late the grave mistake they made in not putting their faith in Him. Then there will be no second chances to get it right.

My faith is strong and only grows stronger as I continue to work and listen to the voice that fills my spirit. When the winds blow, and the rains fall out of the sky, when the thunder cracks open the skyline and the seasons change, it is abundantly clear that nature's living colors come from Heaven. A fire that is completely out-of-control will burn until the area is clear. The recent devastating fires in California provide all too real examples for the hundreds of people who lost their homes, and even their lives.

I do not know how long a time passage is. I expect that it can vary. My time passage for my tenth visit to Brazil was ten weeks. I enjoyed every moment of my time and I wrote until this book was finished.

The people there know me and know my story. They know the "before" me, when I drank, and the new, sober me. They know the gift I have been given. My new life. When you think you have nothing to offer, think again.

I once read a book written by Dr. Charles Stanley. Elisabet and I were on our cruise, when I wrote my second book, <u>On a Mission of Nutrition</u>. I was inspired by Dr. Stanley's book, <u>Waiting on God</u>. I started writing and could not stop. Sometimes, I thought I was dreaming. Four days later, the book was finished. Inspiration is real. God is real. Heaven is real. Elisabet and two other passengers onboard witnessed it unfold. It was amazing!

Even Jesus had to deal with human limitations. He needed sleep. He needed food. He had to escape the crowds. He needed to be alone to pray and communicate with His Father.

There will be many rivers to cross in one's life. We will constantly be searching for solid ground. Sometimes we will struggle to find it. Find the right place to build an unshakable foundation for your life that cannot be torn down. Root it with God's seed and it will stand.

The scriptures hold all the answers to every question we will ever have. We may read through a single passage in the Bible a dozen times on a dozen different days and each day we will find a different meaning in that same passage. God speaks to us through His Word. At times we will not understand what we are reading. Pray. Ask for understanding and it will be given to you. Maybe not immediately, but it will come. Find a Bible translation that works for you.

God's fire burns very hot. When the fire is on you (do not worry, it is not the kind of fire that will actually burn you), you may not realize it the first time. It is a surreal experience. It may occur often or only once in a lifetime. I know this feeling very well. I have it today. I hope that I still feel it tomorrow.

Joseph Esposito

Words are powerful. In scripture, the tongue is called a sword; even a double-edged sword because words can cut both ways. The words we speak can be harmful. They can damage others; they can damage us. We may choke on our own words if we are not careful.

Using God's name in vain is a violation of the Ten Commandments. People do this all the time. Carelessly. Without thinking. It is not a small thing. God's name is Holy. He is to be revered. His name holds power. It is not a curse word and it is not to be called upon casually or flippantly.

Surprises in life pop-up all the time. Not all surprises are good. I like to think that God is watching me and protecting me. I believe His hand is upon me. There is evidence for it in my past. I had two accidents in Brazil. The first was my bicycle accident in 2011. The second was during a sparring match in 2016. I was kicked hard in the right side of my chest by a sixteen-year-old student. I could not breathe for about two minutes and I thought I was surely going to die on the floor of the Academia Tokyo school where I trained.

Had that same kick been in the center of my chest, it could very well have broken my chest and I would have died instantly. Had that same kick been on the left side of my chest, it likely would have stopped my heart instantly and I would have died. Until the day appointed for our death, we can become injured or ill, but we will not die. That kick served as a wake-up call for me. I was severely bruised, but I lived.

We have angels who protect us. The Bible speaks about the existence of angels. For the most part, they are unseen, moving about on a plane that we cannot see. But occasionally they make themselves known. An angel appeared to Mary to let her know she would bear the Messiah, and to Joseph to let him know Mary had conceived by the Holy Spirit. The Bible tells us we may entertain angels, not knowing that they are angels.

Time passages are all around us. Above us in the sky. Below us in the oceans. Beside us in a parallel universe we cannot see, where supernatural battles take place between angels and demons.

Chapter Nine

THIS TIME

*P*roverbs 3:1: My son, do not forget my law, But let your heart keep my commands;

This time is my time. My tenth time in Brazil provided the opportunity to write this book, while I had the fire within me. I accepted it for what it was. I listened carefully to the voice that spoke within me. I do not have times like that when I am home in Connecticut, only when I am somewhere else. I do not know why.

This time may also be your best time. Or it may come later. Will you know it when it comes? Or will you miss the opportunity because you are distracted? We become discouraged when we are not working toward the purpose God intended for us. When we become distracted with things that are unimportant or our thoughts stray into negative areas, we can find ourselves overloaded with unnecessary and unproductive stress. We can then become frustrated, stagnant, unproductive, irritable, and even angry.

Staying focused is imperative in order to operate at an optimum level and achieve the goals we set. We want to maintain forward progress. We want to keep our energy moving in the right direction.

I find that I write the best when my music is blasting through the headphones. Outside noise and distractions are eliminated. I am able to enter that creative zone when I listen to music. I can hear God's voice encourage and inspire me. It is even better if the rain pours down as I write. Inspiration seems to flow with the downpour of tears from Heaven. Writing while it is raining is especially relaxing for me. It washes everything clean and I sense a greater clarity and bond with my Lord and Savior.

Time is everything. Without time, no one can create or achieve anything. As the clock ticks, I write. I find my way home – not to a physical place – but home in my mind; my being. It is a comfortable place. The road here has had many twists and turns. I have gotten lost several times. But I found my way. I think we have to first get lost in order to find our way. God is waiting to help you find your way. You need Him. He will help show you the way, then give you the key to finding inner peace.

A child is a treasure from God, our Lord and Savior Jesus Christ. Jesus came into the world as a child in human flesh just like us. With one huge difference – He was born to save the world from sin. We cannot save ourselves from sin. Only He can, if we put our faith in Him.

We are all connected in this life, even if we may not think so. Despite the different languages and different countries, it was all once connected, before the flood. Everything began anew with Noah and his family. When the flood waters receded, the continents formed. Oceans were created, along with rivers and lakes and streams.

For me, writing is a magical process that brings everything together. It is a precious, priceless gift. When I write I feel that my mind is free, my heart is open, and I am at one with the entire living universe. I feel close to the Creator. I traveled round and round in a lot of circles to get here, covering the same ground – or at least what felt like the same ground. But I did learn a lot along the way, so it was worth it in the end.

Our planet is a mixed bag of violence and greatness. It comes together and breaks apart. It meshes and clashes. Sometimes it seems as if only the strong and crazy will survive and move on.

There is never going to be perfection in this lifetime. It is forbidden to happen.

If you seek perfection, that is a good quality to have, but the process will leave you drained of your energy and it still will never be perfect.

What seems perfect to one will not seem perfect to another. There will always be someone who will do things better than you, or differently than you. Be concerned with your own actions and your own journey. The accomplishments of others are not a threat to you unless you allow them to be.

Life's experiences will always become your greatest teacher.

Schools can be overrated because if your teacher is not smart or having an off day, as teachers do because they are only human, and make many mistakes, then you will struggle learning what they are trying to teach you.

On the other hand, if you are in a great school where the teachers are screened and tested on the knowledge that they have, then the learning process will be much better, but it will never be simple.

Knowledge can be very powerful but when our light gets dimmer and our battery is getting weak, our signal gets lost and that is when you are most vulnerable to make a wrong turn and begin to lose your grip on reality.

I don't believe anyone tries to get lost or lose hope, it happens to some of the brightest and even richest people on this planet. You aren't the only one who feels like that.

While you are still breathing, there is always hope. So breathe deep and get up and start over.

Embrace the new day that has been given to you and dig down deep while you are still standing on solid ground. (I don't mean the dirt.)

Replant yourself and allow room for growth so you can become rooted once again and win the fight this time.

Joseph Esposito

There is a feast waiting for you, but until you can bring yourself to the table, you will go hungry.

Where I came from is not even close to Brazil, and I am not referring to a physical distance. I have come far from the old me to the new, with the help of God. The journey has been an emotional one. When I embraced Jesus Christ, I experienced an immediate overload of emotion – a release – and tears streamed down my face. I felt that God was so near to me that He might even be touching me. It was overwhelming. I have experienced that same feeling many times since, like when I am writing. I feel Him close. I embrace those precious moments.

While writing this book, the connection to Him was strong and the words flowed quickly. I could not type fast enough. God's speed is untouchable and unseen, but it can be felt if we let ourselves be open to His presence.

If Brazil is not one of the Seven Wonders, then it must be the eighth wonder of this world. I can remember my very first time, in 1996, when Elisabet first brought me to meet her parents. I was not the same person I am now. I was not a bad person, but I believe that I am a better person now than I was then.

Becoming free from our old self will never be easy, but with God's help we can crush our demons. Let yourself be fully aware of Him. Let Him walk with you, and you will be just fine.

Chapter Ten

Time Exposes

Proverbs 6:23: For the commandment is a lamp, and the law a light; Reproofs of instruction are the way of life,

Time exposes everything. Our faults, desires, habits, and all the good works that we do will be exposed to the light of day. We can try to run, but we can never hide from the truth that awaits us. Time exposes the truth of even the greatest liars and masters of manipulation.

Books are written every day. That does not mean they are real or true unless they are such as this marvel that God has chosen me to write. We will never have to apologize if we speak the truth.

Giving in to sin will keep us in a place where we are not supposed to be. Keeping our tongues under control and not inviting argument takes practice. Allowing another's words to roll off of us instead of inciting a riot in our minds requires discipline.

We humans are prone to bending the truth in at least small ways at least sometimes. We try to be something we are not. We tell little white lies to make people like us, or think we are somehow more interesting than we really are.

Exposure, good or bad, can make or break us. Trying to put ourselves back together again, particularly if trust has been lost, may be difficult. No one wants to be a fool, and no one likes a foolish person.

Joseph Esposito

I have made so many mistakes in my life. I have lived a foolish lifestyle for so long. After a while, one can get tired of being tired. Then comes the tedious process of cleaning up the messes one has left behind if that is even possible.

If we drive a car down a one-way street in the wrong direction, one of two things will happen: either we will crash into oncoming traffic or we will be extremely lucky. Accidents happen, but sometimes accidents are not really accidents. Sometimes a person drives into a crowd of people on purpose. Unfortunately, today, that has become a terrorist tactic. With terrorists lurking everywhere, in all of our cities, it is impossible to know who they might be in every case. They are violent and intelligent killers who do not like us. Everything happens for a reason. Even these types of things. And our hearts go out to those who suffer because of these cruel and random acts of violence. As time exposes the enemy, we need to stay alert and be prepared to fight them at any given moment.

The truth can never lie. Only people tell lies, for their own gain. Time is not our friend; it is our teacher. Wake up. Enough is not enough for many of us. Misery loves company. I have had my fill of brokenness and pity parties. It is time to rise up above my own carnage and teach what I have learned along my own bumpy, broken road.

It is not hard to be nice to others when you are nice to yourself. Great things happen to nice people most of the time, though not all of the time. A whisper of words will get more attention than a loud mouth. (I tend to talk loudly most of the time. I do not mean to. It is just the way I talk. I guess when and if I make it to a stage someday, my voice will be heard!)

One must be willing to move a crowd with the gift they have received. There will always be hope for deliverance if one is ready to be delivered.

Being exposed can and will be shameful and painful. It is easy to fall from grace. It just may not be easy to get back up. As tears fall from our face, as we feel sick inside, and everything is crashing around us, as it is hard to make sense of anything anymore, that is when we hit the bottom of the barrel. There is only one thing left to do, but we are afraid to admit our faults still. Our secrets are not secrets anymore. Time has taken its toll. We have been called out on our lies.

Giving ourselves time to repent and confess might be a good beginning. Both are necessary to begin to rise out of our mess. When someone has lived a life of sin, deep down inside they have no love for themselves or others. It is a lonely existence. We were not born to live that way.

Appreciate what you have. When you are feeling sorry for yourself, try thinking about someone you know whose circumstances are worse than yours. If you cannot think of anyone, go to a local soup kitchen or homeless shelter and volunteer for an hour or two. Helping others will give you a natural boost. It will take the focus off your own problems.

People born with disabilities, even severe ones, or who learned to adjust to and overcome limitations life unexpectedly threw at them often do not feel sorry for themselves or seem to be limited in ways that we would expect. God often gifts them with extraordinary abilities, grace and strength. Look at Stevie Wonder, for example. Blind, but a gifted and world-renowned singer and songwriter, blessed with enormous joy. There are so many other examples.

Choose to be happy every day that you wake up. It is a choice. I want to watch my grandson grow up. I want to teach him what I have learned in my lifetime. He is a gift. There is nothing greater than the gift of new life. It provides us with a motivation like no other.

We are all uniquely made. We are supposed to get wrinkles, or gray hair, or go bald (in my case). Well, I still have a little hair, I guess. Time exposes our age, and what we will do with that process. Natural beauty needs no cover. Unless we have cancer and are trying to cover up the ravages of that process, which is understandable – that is altogether different.

Someone needs to know the time. I am glad that I am here. This is our clock calling us to get up and get on with our life while we are still able. Chances do not last forever, but regrets do. We have all said, at least once in our lives, that we want to start something. But then we stop. Why is that? Walking around with more weight (physical, emotional, financial) than we want to carry is only going to slow us down. Eliminating it is up to us.

Feelings that live in our hearts and minds, even physical feelings like pain, can be an enemy who drags us down and influences how we will feel on any given day. But only if we let him. Time exposes who we are and what we have become.

All the time, every day, thoughts come and go through our minds. Some we listen to and some we dismiss. Some replay over and over, threatening to drive us mad. Planning one's day includes setting that one goal we think is most important and planning how to achieve it. If one cannot harness one's thoughts enough to focus, this simple task may seem impossible.

If we do not break our bad habits, our habits may break us. All the time we hear people talk about losing weight, quitting smoking, or stopping some other bad habit. How are we going to establish good habits if we cannot get away from our bad habits? Running away from the truth will only keep us from our best destiny. Break the barriers that are holding you back. If you need a spark of energy, ignite a fire within.

Open your eyes and take a good look around you. Accept your situation as it currently is, good or bad. Then do something about it. Emotions can get in our way. Do not allow them to control you. Put them where they belong. Use them for good; do not let them abuse you.

Holding on to negative thoughts will not provide clarity. It will not help us better understand or move past problems. Address problems head-on and resolve issues as quickly and quietly as possible. Staying quiet has always been one of my biggest faults. Making a big deal out of something small only creates a worse scenario. I know.

Coming out of our own closet may never happen if we do not open the door. Staying in the moment long enough will allow time to think and navigate through that process of elimination. All the time we should be learning. All the time we should be doing. All the time we should be thanking God for the time He has given us to progress and become greater than we were yesterday.

Stop denying yourself. You are good enough and you are capable. You are so much stronger than you think you are. Strength does not always have to be physical. Your brain and your heart are your strongest qualities – the ones that cannot be seen but are felt and heard. One without the other will not get us very far.

Being smart and staying smart can become challenging with too much negativity around us on a daily basis. I write with my headphones on so that I can tune into my thoughts without distraction while I listen to positive music of my own selection. The right music moves the soul and soothes the mind. I see music as bits and pieces of carnage from another's soul. That is why it can speak to us on such a personal level. Writing is similar, just without the beat.

Every day, while so many bad things continue to happen in this world, positive things are happening as well. Positive messages are all around us, if we only open our eyes and hearts to see them. The news tells us about the bad people, and the things they do, every day. But there are far more people doing good things everywhere. Look for them and you will see.

I am stubborn. I have been my whole life. I would much rather struggle with something than ask for help. I also do not read directions. I open a box and bypass the instructions on how to put something together or get it to work. Even the "quick-start guide" is asking too much. I am an idiot and I never learn. Before long, I am reading the trouble shooting guide. Time is everywhere. We use it; we lose it; we give it away.

God gave us His time to share and care for His people. His people includes our brothers and sisters who are not related to us by blood. Are we doing that?

We always want what we cannot have but we do not want to do the work required to have what we want. I am always happy when I get what I want or think I need, at least for a moment. But then many times, after I have gotten it, I let it sit without using it. Like all the exercise equipment in my basement. I had to have it. There is something about the feeling of spending money to get something we want. Money is only paper. It comes and goes unless you are a hoarder and not a spender. We have to address that feeling and break that cycle. Saving money is crucial to our future. Learn to become life-wise. Time is passing us by every moment of every day.

Chapter Eleven

A Matter of Time

Proverbs 5:22: His own iniquities entrap the wicked man, And he is caught in the cords of his sin.

It's only a matter of time, once we have figured out the true faults blocking us, to get out of our own way. Only you know how you feel. Knowing how to relieve what is ailing us, however, may be a bit more complicated. Achieving mind over matter is a life-long process. Once we have claimed our "secret within," we will have mastered our inner voice. It is a shame and a pity when we are down on ourselves. We become our own greatest enemy to success.

Creating a new beginning takes time. Money is not the hurdle one has to be concerned with. Millionaires are not the only ones who can make progress. Our greatest asset is deep inside us, not our wallet. What will we do tomorrow, to change what we did not do today? Only we can turn the page in the book of our life.

Creation has no boundaries. Nature is limitless and so are we unless we limit ourselves. Step into life and do not look back. Looking back will only lead us backwards. Schedule time with yourself first. Allow your own freedom first before you share your time with someone else. Time is a gift. Do not waste it anymore.

Joseph Esposito

Look up and look around. Keep both feet planted firmly on solid ground. We can turn our world around. We can bring back happy days and learn to celebrate life again. We are worth celebrating.

Reclaim the energy you had in your youth. I have a theory that we are all born with disease, especially cancer. Some get cancer and others do not because of some sort of damage that we cause internally, without even knowing it. I know that might sound foolish, but no one else seems to know why either. "God giveth and God taketh away."

Our life is a river of dreams and there will be many rivers to cross to get to the other side where we will leave all of our fears behind and take the plunge into new life. Being honest with ourselves may be the hardest thing to come to terms with. Fighting with oneself is something we all do (my wife has been telling me that for a long time and I finally understand), sometimes daily. Listening to oneself is something we need to learn to do. We need to silence the voices of others telling us what is best for us (it is easy to hear those), and really listen to our own voice, maybe for the first time.

Getting in shape and staying in shape are two completely different things; very different. Getting in shape is hard work and mentally challenging. Staying in shape is a habit that will take years of dedication.

Water is toxic on this planet, even if it comes from a bottle. I purchased a Kangen water machine over a year ago and the difference is astonishing. It produces a type of alkaline water that tastes great. I think my energy is improved as a result. The word Kangen means to return to origin. It is a Japanese word and the machine is manufactured there but is available in the United States.

Resist or reside with your own condemnation. It has always been a matter of time which direction we will choose to define our ability to communicate at a higher level with all of mankind. If you are fortunate enough, as I have been, to receive important information and be guided through this type of writing process.

The Gift of Light

A writer is not born.
A writer is gifted.
When a heart is broken,
The spirit is lifted.
When the words come from up above,
It's God's way of showing His love.
As a child of God's light,
Only God's Spirit can make everything bright.
I know you are here because I am still awake.
I really could use more than three hours sleep.
But Your words come so fast and run so deep.
I will give You my promise to share Your words and always keep.
I know Your Spirit is surreal,
Because it's Your powerful force that I always feel.
Even though Your power is never seen,
I get Your message and really know what You mean.
But I really need to get more sleep.
You already know my soul is Yours to keep.
Your powerful gift of light.
Why does it always come so late at night?
Joseph Esposito © 1/11/2018

Joseph Esposito

My Gift is Your Word

My gift is Your Word.
My ears have finally been opened and now I have heard
Your words to me, always soft-spoken when said.
It's Your voice that rings and stays in my head.
I know it's only just a matter of time,
Because it's Your voice that always stays in my mind.
Your powerful words of wisdom and joy;
It's Your voice that I choose to employ
To take me to another place and time.
Your poetry is always second to none.
A new journey into Your fire I shall run.
Your words always come to me so easy and strong.
They come to me in the night and even as the day is long.
With Your powerful words I shall hold within;
As I am here I just wait for You to begin.
Just as Your beauty is seen all around,
With the only exception You are still not to be found.
Joseph Esposito © 1/11/2018

The Best is Yet to Come

Into Your arms as I start to run,
Because You have already told me that the best is yet to come.
I know there is not one love or human stronger than You.
I know there is no one here that can do what You do.
I am always ready as I chose to give up my fight.
You have been telling me now for many years
That so many choose still the dark instead of Your light.
My heart has always been open to You.
I was tied down for so long I just did not know what to do.
Now that Your voice has finally broken through,
Though I lost so much time, I will do what You want me to.
Because I have been chosen and have not been found,
You were always here but I was never around.
Just as You have called me many times before,
I did not know, so I chose to ignore.
But now once again that I have been connected,
You give me new life just as You Yourself have been resurrected.
I know deep inside that I have already won,
Because You tell me still that the best is yet to come.
Joseph Esposito © 1/11/2018

Chapter Twelve

SOMEWHERE IN TIME

Proverbs 3:35: The wise shall inherit glory, But shame shall be the legacy of fools.

Somewhere in time we are going to pick up our pieces and start flowing in the new moment. Staying and living in the flow stream of universality is something that comes naturally when we are connected to the unseen energy that is flowing. Keeping up with the new flowing energy is going to become our new habit. Being able to receive and transmit that same energy to the new connections we make along our journey requires time and the right words.

Energy never stops, whether seen or unseen. Most energy comes at a cost. Universal energy is free but requires the ability to tap into the unseen energy that is all around us. The universe sends out waves of energy, similar to the way the ocean sends waves of water to lift one up on a surf board and carry one to the beach. (Learning to surf is another matter entirely, taking a strong body and a keen sense of balance and stability. Once achieved, the feeling of riding a wave on a board is a whole new world of fun!)

The universal wave of unseen energy is very different. We cannot touch it or see it. We can, however, feel it when we are in its constant flowing stream. Once we have found it, we will want to get inside and stay there. It is magical.

The universe is full of unseen power that only a select few will be able to tap into themselves. Most people will seek a coach or mentor. Mine has always been the Word of God. His teachings are superior; the scriptures provide the necessary knowledge to take one there.

Knowledge is power, and power is everywhere, in many shapes and forms. Knowing the difference is imperative to know how to find the power that allows us to create energy from within our own mind and body, and even more energy for our soul. Once we have found the perfect combination of powerful energy, we must learn to focus, contain and control this new energy.

Energy and power are spontaneous, fast bursts of frequent moments in time. As the seconds click away, energy is doing the same thing. It disappears without our awareness. Why? We do not think of energy as a source of supernatural power. We are not like our creators, and hence the creators of all energy.

Control is key. It is okay to be excited but getting carried away with the new excitement we have found can and will have consequences. (Like having too much money all at once, where our spending can quickly get out of control.) Because this is new energy that we have not had before, we must learn to control it. Coaches and mentors are one option, which may work for some but not others. This is also an option ripe for scam artists, so be careful and do your research if you choose to pay someone to help you.

My mentor has been God. His services and guidance are free. His advice is always true, though my ability to hear Him may not always be without interference. Hence it has taken me time and not a few mistakes to get to the place I am today. We cannot learn everything in life from books or school. Somewhere in time we become "life-wise" to help ourselves along our way.

Every time someone says I am not smart enough or brave enough or some other criticism to knock me down, it only adds fuel to my fire to succeed. With one exception these days, I choose to do what is right instead of what is wrong. I crush the negative with a positive. I tune out the criticism and listen to the voice deep inside of me that tells me I can; that tells me I am in charge of my life and my choices. The negative naysayer is not in control here anymore.

Your time is your own, when it is your time! Somewhere in time, when you do not need to fight with yourself anymore; when you do not need to overthink things anymore; when you can stop retaliating to and replaying every negative comment, you will know you have made the decision to stop blocking yourself from moving forward. Somewhere in time you will get what you need. You know how to get it.

Some things in life come easy. Some things are given as a gift. Life is a gift. For most, every day above ground is a good day. We should not waste any day. We might not have tomorrow.

If we are still able to breathe on our own; if we are still able to hear the birds sing; if we are still able to see the sun rise and set, we should be thankful. Our senses and abilities will decrease and may even be taken away with age, illness and injury. We can and should take care of ourselves to the best of our ability, avoiding unnecessary risks. Some of us will. Many of us will not. We know the potential costs.

Faith and hope go hand in hand. If we have the desire to change, and the will to change, what we know is wrong in our lives and the way we live them, we can do anything. The first step is a big one. It requires a giant leap of faith out of what might otherwise be a hopeless situation. Find the courage to do something. Act on what you believe is holding you back. Take the first step in a positive direction. The first step is the most difficult. Always. The first step is a requirement before the second step is even possible. Be strong. You can do it.

Just stand up and let go. Move your feet. Listen to God. You will have set-backs. Do not let them stop you or turn you around. Keep going. It is a long journey. Find God's light and let it light your path.

If you live a broken life because of a broken household or a traumatic event or an addiction or for any other reason, find the love of God – the only true love – and let it set you free from your brokenness. I lived a broken life. As a child, everything was taken away from me because my parents divorced. My father sold the only house that I had known as my home. The consequences of that followed me around, haunted me, blocked me. Until I let God set me free with His love. We will not find that kind of love in the world. Only in God. He is not just somewhere in time, He is everywhere in time.

Chapter Thirteen

Time Table

Proverbs 8:14: Counsel is mine, and sound wisdom; I am understanding, I have strength.

Time tables are a way of life. We are taught times tables in math class in school as children. We learn about denominations and multiplications; how to add and subtract and divide.

Our life is only a number, not the name we are given at our birth. When Jesus calls our number, we will be gone. Which time table we choose to live by on earth may determine which table we sit at in Heaven.

There are tables all around us, everywhere. As a child we sit at a table with our parents to eat our meals. We play games at tables, like pool or ping-pong. Some of these tables are at clubs and bars, places where we are also enticed with potentially addictive habits. Just because we are in these places does not mean we will succumb, but the temptation beckons.

If and when we make one of these places our destination hangout – the more and more of our time we spend there – without conscious thought, we are making it easier and easier for a time stealing addiction to take over our life and become a major player in our personal time table.

Joseph Esposito

Gambling could be next. Sitting at a card or craps table in a casino, laying down money we may not have, drinking more and more alcohol to calm our anxiety, eventually taking on debt to cover our losses. Who have we become? What has this time stealing time table done to us? What have we done to ourselves? We cannot stop. We tell ourselves that we have to keep going because the only way out is through – to try to win our money back. Except that we never will.

I know only too well. I spent too much time and money playing games in casinos all over the United States. I was invited to stay in Atlantic City, Las Vegas, Mohegan Sun and Foxwoods so many times. Free rooms and free food. Except it is not free. They know your players card will go into a slot machine in their casino. They know you will sit at their tables and spend money. They know they can track your play and bank your losses.

The casinos are rich and powerful and greedy. They are in business to make money. They will let you win to get you hooked, but in the end, you will lose. The tables will turn on you. They always do. If you have gotten yourself off track and as the tables turn on your life, you have a decision to make. This is where you will learn or burn.

There are four critical qualities all people develop early in life, depending on the influences of the people around them, their experiences, and their inner strength: (1) character; (2) conversation; (3) conduct; and (4) control. If you have the first three well-in-hand and were fortunate enough to have developed them as you grew up, unlike myself, you are probably doing great things already and your life is not a train wreck.

If we have not attained a level of maturity with regard to character, conversation and conduct by the time you reach adulthood, then we have work to do. It is likely that our life is messy at best in one or more of these areas. We cannot begin to work on control until we clean up the first three.

Control is the biggest of the four. I am learning how to control the things around me as well as the things inside me. This includes controlling my temper, my spending habits, my eating habits, and my desires. It is important to find and maintain balance to achieve an abundant and healthy lifestyle.

We are our greatest asset. Finding our true value in life may take a very long time. Once we know what it is, we can start sharing it with others. Those who really know us and care about us likely knew our true value before we did. Strangers are another story altogether. Some will want to know us; others will never care who we are.

Friends come and go. Families can fall apart. Loved ones and friends pass away. Only God is always there. Even when we are alone, we are never really alone if we let God in. Learn to appreciate the quiet times when you are alone. Listen to the voice that whispers in your soul. God is speaking. You will hear Him if you block the distractions that are constantly trying to interrupt. Learn to listen – really listen.

The sun will rise in the morning. We can rise and shine as well. There is a danger in loving someone too much. Sometimes love may not be enough. We let ourselves get hurt and then we carry the baggage of that hurt around with us. It gets heavier and heavier the longer we carry it. We use it as an excuse to not open our hearts up again to someone else because we hold on to the pain of our broken heart. We hold it for so long we forget the joy of a heart in love.

Love is powerful and opens us up to the possibility of pain. Love is not always equally given or received. There are different types of love. The selfless love of a parent for a child; romantic love; God's love for us. God's unconditional love is the touchstone.

Time tables are measured by more than just numbers. Once we are aware of the various games people play we will be better able to navigate through them unscathed. God creates winners; we were not born to lose at life. Nothing is impossible, especially if we cling to Him. We lose at life's time tables because of poor choices and too many excuses. Wake up. Do not wait for the tables to be turned on you. Turn your own table.

Chapter Fourteen

Your Time

Proverbs 10:4: He who has a slack hand becomes poor, But the hand of the diligent makes rich.

Your time is only your own time when it is your time. I never liked punching a clock or working for someone else. Being self-employed has its benefits. When we are our own boss, we have better control of our time. There are also many disadvantages. Because we are the boss, when things go wrong we are the one who must fix them. If the fixes are costly (in time or money), the cost comes out of our bottom line, not someone else's. If we need employees to help us get things done, we must hope that they are honest and diligent workers. We have to ensure they are trained and qualified. Our success may depend on several factors that are our responsibility but are out of our direct control. No one will care about our business as much as we will.

Many people get caught up in the time warp of working for others, at a job they hate. They go to work only because they have to work. Working for someone else can be rewarding if we are doing something we love to do; if we are working for someone we admire and respect, who treats us well.

Some are lucky enough to identify their dream job at an early age, attend school to prepare for that job, and actually find work in that field. Some common examples come to mind: marine biologists, firemen and veterinarians.

Others fall into a career field by accident or process of elimination. The result may be a happy one or not. Some get a job because it is expected based on their geography, such as the auto or coal industries. If one lives in that location and is able-bodied, it is expected that one will take care of one's family by entering that particular industry. Still others get whatever job they can get, sometimes over and over again.

Our time may be spinning out of control while we struggle at work to get a job, keep a job, make money, make more money, and study on the side for a better job. Jobs may come and go. Positions get kicked along with the people as companies come and go and as technologies change. We may lose our job. Maybe we deserved to; maybe we did not. The result is the same. When one loses a job, the stress can be catastrophic.

How will we handle it? Will we get up tomorrow and look for another job? Or will we spiral downward and become a fixture at the local bar, wallowing in self-pity? We may have never thought it could get this bad but here we are again. Unemployed for one reason or another.

In a certain light, we all look the same. It might be the dark light of shame and self-doubt or the bright light of God's love that will hold us up no matter our circumstances. Which will you choose?

If you choose the first, you are riding the all-night train, thinking and drinking and hoping tomorrow the phone rings with a job offer you do not think you deserve. The rent is past due, and the credit cards are over the limit. You drank away the only cash you had left.

If you choose the second, you will hold your head up and see your worth. You will put down the beer and get some sleep because tomorrow you have work to do. You will get yourself cleaned up and start working on a plan. If no one is hiring you will find out what you can do to work for yourself. You have skills. It is your time. You will use it.

Good timing creates opportunities and we control our time. We can make the most of our circumstances, regardless of what they are. Luck, good or bad, has nothing to do with the outcome. Press onward. Work hard. Think positive. Take control of your destiny. Nothing is accomplished by giving up or quitting. Follow through even if it hurts.

We do not appreciate those things that are given to us half as much as we appreciate what we work hard to accomplish ourselves. Invest your time in yourself and make the most out of your time. You may be surprised at what happens!

Chapter Fifteen

NEXT TIME

*P*roverbs 8:13: The fear of the Lord is to hate evil; Pride and arrogance and the evil way And the perverse mouth I hate.

Next time you find yourself filled with a mindset of self-doubt, banish it far away. Do not let it haunt you and fill you with anger. I have to fight that tendency myself. Toxic words can create a venomous relationship with others. Be cognizant of what you say, before your words poison treasured bonds among family and friends and derail professional associations.

Venom can be felt from the bitterness of another's negative mindset and their negative actions. Poisonous venom normally comes from a snake bite. I believe toxic venom can come from people, places and things, similar to foods that are laced with toxic chemicals that can slowly poison our bodies. Venom is tasteless. Like a snakebite, it can get in our bloodstream and kill.

Doctors prescribe all kinds of medications that have side effects. Many of these do not show up until months or even years later. Some can kill us. What is supposed to help us or cure us can ultimately kill us.

We can ingest or inhale tasteless, odorless venom through our mouths or nostrils. It can invade our bodies, permeating every part of us, infiltrating our organs and intestines. We may not notice any symptoms until it is too late.

Venom is everywhere: television, radio, newspapers, magazines, billboards, the Internet. Even our conversations, seemingly innocuous, can contain toxic venom. We are so inundated with it we do not even see it or hear it any more. It comes out of our own mouths too. Stop. Really look. Really listen. We can see it. We can hear it. If we try. We must try.

Listen to what comes out of our own mouths. Listen to how toxic our own words are without even thinking about what we say, or how we sound, or who we are talking to. We have stopped caring how we sound. Toxic is as venom does. Spreading rumors or gossiping about others is toxic. It does not matter if what we are saying is true or not. Talking behind the back of others is harmful, toxic. Stop. If we could taste our words they would be unpleasantly bitter or sour.

Conversations should engage the parties and consider their feelings. There is so much to share and so many people to share with. We have much to gain by learning from the experiences of others and much to give by extending our life-lessons to others who want to benefit from them. The world is a rich cultural buffet, but we have to remove the toxic venom from our exchanges. Many people walk around with their eyes open, but they are not awake. They smile, but they are angry inside. They pretend to be alive, but they are dead inside. The venom flows in their bloodstreams. I know. I was one of them for a long time. Fortunately, I broke free. I found the anti-venom: God. My mind is open. I am aware and connected to a higher, supreme power.

South America, especially Brazil, is one of the places I feel most closely connected to God. It has such a natural beauty. Something very special happens to me when I am there. I feel God's presence so much stronger in my life. I realize how much we take for granted and how important it is for people to wake up. We are given but one life. It is meant to be lived.

We die a little more each day. We cannot revive the time that has passed. We look in the mirror and see the effects of the passage of time in our face. Our youth has slipped away. It is not too late to create new memories. To make our life count.

Getting good with God starts with ourselves. We need to understand how our Creator works to be able to live as He wants us to live. To understand Him, read His Word, the Bible.

Music can fill us with inspiration, touching our senses and memories on a deep level. Most of us have music playing while we drive, while we exercise, and while we do many other activities. As we listen to music we are transported in our minds to other times and places through the memories that are evoked. Music is powerful.

In a similar way, we can find inspiration everywhere we look. We can see evidence of creation in every mountain range, every sunrise and sunset, a rainforest, and even the movements of a simple frog. We take photographs of everything to commemorate various events in our lives, some momentous, some trivial. Every picture tells a story and brings back a memory of a certain time, event, thing or person. Except when we are robbed of our memories by disease, memories last a lifetime. Good memories are the most precious, but even the bad ones remain, though we can choose to push them into our memory archives where they are not so persistently painful.

Our problems are our own. But if we join hands and walk forward together, we can leave those troubles behind. We can move forward and choose to not look back. We can start all over again. Maybe someday we will be able to live our lives out loud. We can run with abandon and put an end to all of our doubts. Next time may be only a minute away if we truly believe it and remember how good it can be.

There is a tiny candle that burns like a flame inside each and every one of us. Wherever our flame goes, we go too. Keep your candle hot. Let God's fire burn like a flame. God's fire is hot, so turn it up.

Starting is beginning and when we do not notice the road blocks in front of us, they will disappear as quickly as they appeared. Whatever we want can be given to us if we know what to do and how to ask for it. Even if we only have half of our breath, we can still change our time if we are still alive.

Our eyes tell our stories. If our fire is going out, our eyes will reveal our pain or our fire. Do not be blinded by another person's wicked ways.

Some dreams come in the night time and some seem like yesterday. It seems like forever because our time runs away even though we are living in the moment. Our time escapes regardless of what day it is. Even though people may change, we need to change too. It will not come easy because time does not stand still. Nor should we stand still.

Open your heart and let us come together. Our world needs us now more than ever. Do not play with your heart. Your feelings are your own.

Live your life in living color. Use your imagination and be creative, even if you only see things in black and white. Forget about race and language. Love your brothers and sisters even if you do not understand what they are saying. It is going to be okay once you are okay.

Do not limit yourself to people, places or things. Be limitless with your emotions and with your gifts. Give back by using your gifts to create. Your gifts make you unique. God may have created us all equal, but we are also very different. We should learn how to love one another for our differences.

Chapter Sixteen

IN TIME

Proverbs 15:28: The heart of the righteous studies how to answer, But the mouth of the wicked pours forth evil.

In time things break no matter what they are. A broken bone must be set properly to heal. Even then, healing takes time. After a surgery, medication is prescribed. The doctor provides detailed information for the patient to follow so that recovery from surgery will be successful. Failure to follow the doctor's orders may have disastrous consequences.

In life, when we fall apart because of hurtful words said or misinterpreted, or maybe even something silly like misplaced keys or a cell phone, we may become irritated or agitated. I know I do. Losing time creates stress. Stress creates friction. Friction creates anger. Anger creates bitterness. A wall of separation quickly rises between ourselves and everything around us. Our energy is drained from our minds and bodies. We stop communicating effectively. We lose control. The wall needs to come down. The sooner the better.

When we get irritated or angry we lose our composure and control. We slip into a momentary madness and stop being able to rationalize situations that should be easy to navigate. Little things become big things in our minds. We let them get in our way and trip us up when we could easily step around them or over them and move on.

This is when it really helps to have a higher power to light the way and give us perspective. We are again able to see things for what they are. We can master our inner critic and temper our thoughts before they get out of control. We can learn to subdue our irrational feelings of anger and irritation that send us to places we would rather not go.

Anything is possible when we know how to think it through. Saying and doing are two completely different things. Actions speak louder than words. Words, when well-spoken, attract attention. When we become upset and say negative things, we also attract attention, but of a different kind. This kind of attention often ends up starting an argument or a fight. Maybe not a physical fight, but one that hurts others nonetheless.

Keeping our channel open, allowing positive energy to flow, is key. Finding the key is the challenge. If we have a lock on a gate and a ring full of keys, we have to find the right key, or the lock will not open. There is also a key that will unlock and open the door to our mind – a door that may have been closed for many years. Success comes when we find the right key. When we are talking about the mind, in particular, keys come in all shapes and sizes. There may be many different keys to open all of the various closed doors that await us.

We were not born yesterday. It took many years and many experiences to get where we are in life. Our minds have been invaded over and over again with good and bad experiences, with memories we treasure and those we would rather forget. Our ears have heard things that have soothed us and hurt us. Our mouths have said things that we are proud of and that we wish we could take back. It can be enough to become wrecked, mentally, spiritually and physically. In time, we learn to forget, or we rise above. Pain runs and ruins our body and controls our thoughts, all at the same time.

Time keeps running. When we are stressed, in a hurry, with limited time, time just keeps running. We hit the drive-through and eat on the run because there is not enough time to do anything else. We race the clock to the airport to catch a flight for a business trip, barely making it to the gate on time.

Imagine what we could do if we could stop the clock and go back to yesterday to do everything over. Imagine if we could take back the words we spoke last week in anger and replace them with words of love. Would it make a difference? What if it is too late?

There are many energy-stealers that instantly deplete our energy. When we are rudely interrupted, we feel irritated or angry and lose our moment of thought. We can burn ourselves out in the gym working out too much (what are we really trying to prove or who are we really trying to impress?). We argue because we misinterpreted what we heard someone say. Take a deep breath. Accept what you cannot change. Cry if you must – it can serve as a great release.

Regain your composure and redirect your thoughts and actions in a positive direction. You can meditate. Meditation can bring a new light to anything if done correctly. Triangulated breathing is another way to calm the mind and reset the nervous system. If you have access to one, spend time under a waterfall. It is breathtaking and will reset your world. Take a swim in a pool or the ocean. Listen to music.

The world is round for a reason – everything is whole when it is in the round. Not so much when things go wrong: one of your car's tires becomes flat and the tire will not roll anymore; your favorite LP record develops a scratch and it now skips over your favorite song on the album; and your circle of friends is broken because they say you are crazy.

Your love is always alive but maybe because of your shattered mind or your broken heart you start to get lost and forget who you once were. Staying beautiful on the inside has nothing to do with appearance. Sure, everyone would like to be more physically attractive. Ugly is a four-letter word that does not just refer to external appearance. People spend too much time looking for beauty on the outside first; they never give a thought that they might be looking at a beautiful ugly person. What is on the inside counts!

Repetitive behavior, good or bad, causes repetitive habits. Our time must bring us to that final destination. Focus and find it.

It is a wild world with many wild animals and wild people too. Some animals are better than people. Many people have been hurt so badly that they simply cannot take another chance in life; they prefer animal companionship to another broken friendship or relationship with people.

We need to be converted, not inverted. Construction creates beauty; destruction destroys. Both cannot stand in the same space. Either we build, or we break.

A rock and roll band plays music that is raw and loud. It is not that the band cannot play soft music or that they do not know how; a true musician can play any kind of music. They have a loud energy. That is what sounds and feels best to them, so that is what they play.

Balance is a big word that starts with our body and then our mind. It branches out to our extended life outside of ourselves. If we have great balance in our body and mind, and if we know how to balance our time, then we are winning. It is all in the way that we use it.

No one is right until someone is wrong. Balance comes and goes. Do not ever lose or abuse your balance. Be careful because when we teeter, we also totter; up and down, back and forth. Keep planting your feet on solid ground.

Choose a positive force with relentless energy and come as you are. Take your time. Hurry up and do not be late. Explosive power without a gun. A charging force of positive activity. We are already equipped to be who we are supposed to be. God made us that way a long time ago, long before we were ever born.

We were born to live in the organic, natural state before mankind corrupted the soil and changed the foods that were once packed with natural nutrients and good for our bodies. God's natural beauty is inside us and all around us.

We cannot fix a hole in the wall or in the ground unless there is a hole there to fix. Like an unseen hole inside our body or mind, the unseen space must be filled before we can become whole again. Like a cavity filled by the dentist, once the hole is repaired, it will heal.

Healing has many definitions. It can be a feeling, like when a person takes candy from a baby. The baby will cry but when the candy is replaced, the baby's feelings are pacified and healed temporarily. Spiritual healing is on a much higher level and priceless. Like anything else, it requires time. Disconnecting everything that we already are to create space for what is to come. Allowing an unseen energy from someone or somewhere. Channeling energy from a light or stone or other natural source in the forest or ocean.

Imagine being rejuvenated with a new energetic power that you never knew existed. The walls we have built around ourselves for so many years have now blocked us from even the possibility of such energies and powers.

On January 17, 2018, I experienced something that I had never heard of before, something called the healing powers of John of God. I went to this place to see it with my own eyes. The next day, January 18, 2018, I returned to have my own four-hour spiritual healing session. Afterward, I waited for the invisible power of the entities that were bestowed inside of my body.

I was told that I had invisible stitches and when I left the grounds that John of God created many years ago and returned home (or to the place where I was staying in Brazil), that I should follow these instructions:

For the first twenty-four hours I was to go directly to bed and rest and sleep. No talking, no electronics, completely disconnect from myself. It was okay to eat and use the bathroom. I was told the first twenty-four hours were very critical. I was given a natural medicine called Passiflora. I was told it is a mineral that grows in a secret garden that God planted thousands of years ago. I also had to believe in

God and John of God or the time I had already spent would have no effect at all.

After the first twenty-four hours, I was not allowed to do any type of physical exercise for the next eight days. This was challenging for me. As a martial artist, I have an abundance of energy and needed to keep moving constantly upon waking up each morning.

My life was turned upside-down. My mind was sent in a different direction – somewhere it had never gone before. I was on an eight-day journey into the light of an unknown, unseen, powerful entity that took control over me.

Opportunities awaited me that I could not anticipate. In the dark of night, and by the light of day, I found myself working twenty-four hours at a time. The experience I had witnessed was like nothing I had ever seen or experienced before. Home sweet home would never be the same. More change was on the way. A new direction. A different level in time. This was another new beginning for me. More fuel had been added to my already hot fire.

I did not know what to expect from one day to the next. People, places and things were full of surprises for me, especially John of God. Another item checked off my bucket list. Each time I come to Brazil I experience great surprises. The John of God experience topped them all. I can only wonder what will be next.

Someday in time I will learn what this all means. God will always be first in my life. Everything else that has happened comes second. The gift that has been given to me is a big one and I must own it. My life is brilliant and pure when I am in Brazil. My energy has always shined like a bright light – one that has mostly driven people away. I am too much to handle even when sober. My conversations are often distorted.

I expected clarity and focus to become astounding. I never doubted the powerful forces that are unseen. I just did not know how to tap in. The John of God experience enhanced and enlightened my new celebration into the spirit world.

Twenty-four hours is always only a day away. I went for a new ride on a journey where I had never gone before. I already know how God's fire is when it is on me. Just like the calm before the storm, another storm was brewing. It was on the horizon and this time I was the storm that was coming. Bringing a new light for the world to acknowledge in time.

Chapter Seventeen

ANYTIME

Proverbs 22:6: Train up a child in the way he should go, And when he is old he will not depart from it.

Anytime is better than no time. Anything can happen at any given moment. That is the greatest thing about time. Something can happen any day or every day we choose.

I did not mind giving up nine days of my time. If I had not gone to the John of God experience, I would have continued in my daily martial arts practice. Since 2010, when I first walked through the doors of the karate school Academia Tokyo, Instructor Geraldo has been more than just my instructor. He has become a close friend. He teaches Shotokan karate and American kickboxing. I have the utmost respect for him, his school, and the other students and instructors. The feelings are mutual. Respect is part of the martial arts discipline. Anytime at Academia Tokyo is time well spent.

But for the remaining eight days following the John of God experience, I hunkered down and studied the martial arts books that Geraldo gave me instead. These allowed me to dig deeper and focus on the finer artistic details of my beloved martial arts.

I have always been passionate and determined but my excitement can distract me from owning what I have learned. My new knowledge could sink in; I had to patiently wait for it. Anytime was in lockdown.

I had to submit to a reclusive state of mind – somewhere I had never been before.

Without a belief system in love and life, no dreams can come to pass. Without the love of God in our heart, our dreams do not come to light. Instead they become shattered and broken and stolen away from us. The beliefs we choose for ourselves, without God, are empty. God is the one thing worth caring about; the one who can make all of our dreams come true.

Blessings come in many forms in this lifetime. God gives us His blessings. He also has the power to take everything away. When God is put first in our lives, magical things can happen. Many people suffer because they lack faith in an unseen entity. Unless and until a change is made, they are on a path of destruction. Happiness without God is an illusion.

Money is dirty paper that gets passed around through the hands of many. Money can take us far, but only for a little while. Chasing paper money will not lead to happiness but it just might lead to hell.

Believing in oneself is amazing. But it is not where most of us find ourselves. Most of us are riding a blue train to nowhere. We have forgotten where we wanted to go in the first place. At some point the track will run out and the train will stop. We will have to get off and we will find ourselves either at a dead end, in the middle of nowhere, or at a crossroads with a choice to make. We can accept that we made bad decisions and we can change direction. Which direction will we go? One leads on the path to hell and destruction. The other into God's warm light and salvation.

Life can become very long and lonely if we are not careful. God will give us all the rope we need to hang ourselves, but He will never put that rope around our neck. Only we can do that. We must choose which way our pendulum will swing as our time is ticking. Choose wisely my friend. Your clock keeps ticking and your life is calling you.

Four things we must do to live a righteous life: sharing, caring, living and giving. A place in your heart will either become the fight of your life or a dream come true. You should be dancing. Wake up happy every day. Do not hide from the sun. It is a gift from God that should be glorified. Enjoy the small pleasures that have been given to you. Get your life back while you have some time left. Redeem your spirit. The rewards you receive will be priceless and limitless.

Our power is not our own, just like our time is not our own. Stay awake. Stay alert. Our awareness is our new power. The enemy is right behind us. Stay busy and the enemy will leave you alone. Do not open the door to hell; live life in the sunlight. Get up. Get out. Most of all, believe in God and yourself.

Our mind is precious and powerful if we have a mind to control and not a mind that is controlling us. Do not be just a number caught up in a time game filled with numbers; a statistical being without a clue. I hope and pray that the message given to me is getting through to you.

Maybe you are one of the fortunate few who have been doing great things your whole life. You have not lost your way. If so, it is people like you that this world can never have enough of. You become the great leaders of the world. You become the ones who make a difference every day.

Jesus is watching and listening and directing and redirecting my steps and your steps too. Step into life. Trust Him. Burn with the fire that has been given to you. Good men and women are hard to find. Be that person. If not for your own sake, for God's sake. Be relentless. Learn to become unshakable with your time.

Do good works my friend. You do not need to be rich. It is not necessary to have a penny to do good. We take nothing with us when we go. We take too much for granted. God can connect with us and use us wherever we are.

Matthew 13:9: "He who has ears to hear, let him hear!"

We do not need money, or even electricity, to appreciate the glories of God's creation. If you are somewhere that you can appreciate nature, go outside. See the beauty that is around you in the trees, a butterfly, a hummingbird. Close your eyes and listen to the sounds of birds singing all around you, water flowing if there is a stream or pond nearby, or even the wind blowing through the leaves of a tree. Take in a deep breath and smell the sweet fragrances of flowers in bloom or crisp, clean air if it is winter or fall. God's entertainment is free. The gift of life is sacred. We have just forgotten how to appreciate it. We have become so wrapped up in our concrete and electronic world that we no longer see, hear, smell and feel the beauty of the natural one around us.

Why do we kill God's creatures and destroy His creation? Why is there senseless cruelty among mankind toward the helpless and innocent? I do not understand. My father-in-law, whom I loved dearly (more than my own father, if truth be told), had a cruel streak toward cats. He never liked them. I love cats. I love cats as much as I love horses. But my father-in-law did not like cats and he would kill them. Early in the morning the cats would climb up on the roof in the back of the house and cry. He would get his gun and shoot them. Then he threw their dead carcasses out in the street. This hurt and pained me so much that I would cry and become angry with him. I once cursed at him, telling him God would punish him with a scorpion sting or another snake bite (he had been bitten by rattlesnakes six different times in his life) if he did not stop killing the cats. I know it was probably a sin to curse him, but I did not understand why or how he could kill those cats.

It is far better to feed the cats and dogs and love the poor and hungry and homeless. Do not worry about the consequences. Just be kind. Jesus was kind. He set the example for us to follow.

Wasted time is the same as dead works. There is no reward for either. Some things in life we cannot change. Do not waste time trying to change things you have no control over. It is a win if you can change yourself. Anytime is twenty-four hours a day. Though there are some who would not agree with that statement.

Will you wait until you breathe your last breath to ask God to stay with you? Why wait? Ask Him now. If we turn our face away from Him in this life, He may turn His away from us when we die. If we wait to ask Him into our life, it just might be too late. Do not wait. Do it now. He is waiting for each one of us to reach out to Him. He is always waiting for us. Our choice about Him makes all the difference in our lives, now and for our eternal futures. But know this, He will not make us choose Him. We can believe in whatever, or whomever, we choose. The choice we make will make all the difference in whether we win or lose.

Yesterday is dead and gone. Tomorrow will take care of itself. Put one foot in front of the other and take that first step now. Love can be an uphill battle. Do not become discouraged because nothing is the way it used to be.

Chapter Eighteen

TIME WORKS WHEN IT'S YOUR TIME

Psalm 89:47: Remember how short my time is; For what futility have You created all the children of men?

Proverbs 19:20: Listen to counsel and receive instruction, That you may be wise in your latter days.

Time works if you know how to work your time. As I sat in Brazil on another extended vacation with very little sleep each night, I still awoke every morning with an abundance of energy and messages hammered into my mind. My wife ridiculed me because of my good behavior. I tried not to get upset at her negativity and lack of faith in Jesus.

I am still amazed at my compulsion to write. It is a passion that has overcome my being. I laughed under my breath and saw it as a test in time. My gift is Your gift. It always has been. I just haven't always been as aware of it as I am now. The words come quickly. I cannot type fast enough. I will run with the messages as long as they keep coming, whatever the cost.

I felt watched for some time now. My acute awareness told me so much more. Only recently I was shaking John of God's hand and taking a photograph with this miracle man. He is controlled by forty different doctors and spiritual healers who have walked this earth before him. All died after living gifted lives. These entities still work in spirit through him because of his magnitude of faith and authentic lifestyle of caring more about others than he does himself.

A writer must have a past. I know that I was chosen to write back in 2011 when I had that catastrophic bicycle accident here in Brazil. The power of God compelled me then, as it does now and has every time I have written. My past is ten years of poor schooling and forty years of living life in the wrong lane. Some of this story is my own but the majority of it is not.

Mediums are all over this planet. They are mostly hidden because of the situations and people they allow themselves to be put in with, like my wife. Every time I open my computer and open my phone, I plug my ears with earphones to drown out the negativity that surrounds me. My time works for me and I must deliver this time, despite what people may think or say. Their thoughts mean nothing. It is not my problem if they cannot understand how the universe works. Ultimately it is their own problem to solve in their own time.

Believe what you want, and I will believe what I always have. I have been chosen to do this for the rest of my days: wake up the sleepy minds that must either wake up or go to sleep forever. This is not a game anymore. This is life in text form and I am the writer. With over six hundred poems to date, mostly religious ones, either prophesying about when Jesus comes or about the power of God, there is ample evidence of an influence beyond myself in my writing.

Time works, just like anything else when I am trying and doing my very best to erase bad memories and desires, ultimately quitting every bad habit that got me here today. The tough love of my daughter was my wake-up call. After gulping down three bottles of strong wine at her engagement party, she told me I needed to change my life or forget my grandson forever. I did not black out. Instead I drove to a bar, blind drunk, crying. I was forced to finally go home when that

Time Escapes

bar closed down. I was lucky not to have been pulled over and arrested that night; or worse, to have hit and killed someone.

God has always watched over me. Even in my youth, someone watched over me when I was foolish. Someone kept steering me, and literally my steering wheel, to a brighter destination. That night when I got home I cried again when I saw the large picture in my living room of Jesus standing there knocking on a door. It is an oil painting that hangs in my mother-in-law's house in a glass picture frame. I fell in love with it the first time I ever saw it. It could always make me cry, seeing the likeness of our Creator trying gently to get someone's attention.

That night, November 13, 2014, I made a promise to my Creator to forever end my temptation to drink. I have kept that promise. I have kept it despite many trips to casinos, two cruises with complimentary alcohol, and several trips to Brazil where my drinking was legendary.

God's spirit is in my blood. I am on a guided path to a calling I cannot wait to fulfill. The love is real on both sides of this fence. I get goose bumps from head to toe several times a day. I have to wipe the tears from my eyes when I tell my story of redemption. My pain is real, and this is how I heal.

People cannot learn in school what I am being taught on a daily basis. It is easy to determine my own story from the rest of the story as it is told. I have a burning desire to speak every chance I get. I am now looking forward to speaking in an Evangelical church in Uberaba, where my pastor friend Flavio is the leader of his own church. Flavio does not yet know it, but when his brother, Dr. Ronaldo takes me there, I will speak at his church where I was re-baptized in 2016. The great thing about having a strong belief system is that the words will be given to you in the moment when you need them. God's power is always there when you show up. His power will allow you to deliver His message.

Quitting is never an option. Quitting only prolongs the agony. I know this first hand since I blocked myself for such a very long time.

Joseph Esposito

This story would not be possible if I was not capable of speaking to a large crowd. I talk to people everywhere I go. Most seem to appreciate my message and that is rewarding to me. "Do unto others as you would have done to yourself." I have absolutely nothing to lose and everything to gain by stepping out of my comfort zone, so I can get comfortable.

The closer you get the closer they will get. The closer you get to God, the closer He is when you ask to receive, or you seek to find, or when you knock on that door. I am knocking. People are out there waiting to hear something new.

Time works all the time. Just as time never stops, it can become very challenging to do our daily tasks necessary to maintain a healthy lifestyle. With all of our good habits in line, stepping into our daily process of eliminating what is not necessary will help us get through the day more efficiently and create an awareness of time spent. We can become completely aware of each moment in time and appreciate how time works for us.

As our new energy starts to work for us, we can remain calm under normally stressful situations. This is a clear sign of alignment with a higher power; of understanding just how time works when it is your time. When it is your time, you will know it is your time. Waiting for the right time may not seem logical but if we are not careful or prepared, we will be setting ourselves up for failure. We all must fail before we can succeed.

If our mind is weak or our body is pained, functioning with full power is simply not possible. When our feelings are distraught, it is nearly impossible to focus. Being careful on rough or unfamiliar terrain can be difficult. We do not know whether to go slow or move quickly to avoid a hazard. We may have to make a split-second decision and the wrong one can be fatal. Our awareness may not be our foresight or our insight, but our instinct. Only when it is your time will you know.

When it is your time, nothing can stop what is about to happen. Will you win? Winning is a lifestyle of recreating and rekindling our fire. Losing is easy when our beliefs are nonexistent. Giving up and quitting go hand-in-hand. When or if we fall into a losing pattern in life, and nothing seems to go right anymore, we can choose to keep ourselves down or we can choose to break free. We can keep ourselves down with our own thoughts and words of self-doubt that play like a broken record. I know, because I have been there.

Not anymore though. I have made a different choice. I choose myself. I live now with scriptures in my head and my heart. I finally know which way is up and which way to go. More important, I know what time it is. It is time to act! Spiritual guidance is very powerful when it is your time to let go and let God lead the way. No more landslides. No more jealousy. No more anger. Stop looking at your neighbor's lawn and water your own grass if you want it to be greener. The grass is only greener on the other side because we are obsessed with the other side and not our own side.

Everything in this life is created equal when we know and believe that God created it that way. Sometimes less is more. We should only take what we need. If we have too much, then we should give something back. Teachers and preachers have a great deal in common, but not all teachers believe. There is danger in blindly trusting someone who is teaching, especially if they are leading us away from Jesus, the greatest Teacher of all.

A preacher who believes with all his heart in the Word of God can become a great asset for our heart, mind and soul. Putting money in a basket in church is fine if that is where you like to put it. There are many ways to give tithes. Sometimes there are thieves within the church – even one of the disciples, Judas, was a thief. Money is the root of all evil in this life. But we need to trust or find some way to give back to the church because God tells us to and it is the right thing to do.

Joseph Esposito

Fire and rain may not be compatible. When it's your time, problems rain down on you and your money goes up in smoke. Being "easy like a Sunday morning" may not come easy, but if we become real with ourselves, we will be easier on ourselves. Doing what is right for ourselves and being a brighter light for others will help. Sometimes we cannot please everyone we meet, we just need to please ourselves. When we are happy, it is easier to make someone else happy.

"Happy is as happy does" and "stupid is as stupid does." The difference between being happy and being stupid is astounding. Most people are not born stupid. Allowing ourselves to be surrounded by stupidity will affect our way of thinking if we are not careful. Being stupid and staying in a stupid situation will never result in anything positive. On the other hand, being surrounded by happy people and joyful circumstances will bring great beneficial experiences and benefits. I do not believe one can be happy being stupid.

Finding your voice and clearing that open space in your mind to make room for what is to come next will be refreshing. Clean your mess. Time works best when it is your time. Rock your own soul with healing time and finally mend inside. Connect with your body and mind. Feel new life.

Strategically find a new road and map out a direction in time to allow freedom. Once we know where we are going, it will be much easier to get there. Just because the world is round does not mean that we have to keep going in circles.

Feeling good naturally is essential to showing others that life is good and that we can live in life's little wonders. Our lives are made in these small hours that still remain. Let your troubles fall behind you. It is the heart that really matters in the end. Do not become just another hand-me-down.

We may start to think that we are never going to make it on our own. When living is not easy, and our troubles are deep, we may just see people not giving us what we need. We may feel lost and broken.

There may be words left unspoken. We may find it difficult to find our way back home. If we are scared and feel like we cannot move, it is important to remember that there is still something left inside of us. Remember that there is still something that we can do. Cry if necessary, but then dry those tears. Get angry if necessary, but then get over it. The negative feelings will just drag us under. We do not need someone else to lift us up.

Other people will try to make our life what they want it to be. They will not give us what we need to succeed; they will give us just enough to keep us down. Other people will do their best to change us or erase us. They want to push us around and push us down.

Our life, no matter how far we have fallen, is not that complicated. We can always be put back together. When we are desperately lonely and feel like we cannot get back to where we once were; when everything is spinning out of control in the wrong direction; and when we start believing it is true, this is when we need to reach down in our pocket and find some hope. It is our time. God is waiting to pull us up.

Chapter Nineteen

Time to Wake Up

Matthew 18:11: For the Son of Man has come to save that which was lost.

When it's time to wake up, signs will be presented to us. However, the visions or dreams that have been given to us may be misinterpreted as something other than our first wake-up call. Time will move on and if we are fortunate, another message will be given.

The Father and The Son

In the beginning, there was only One,
A Creator known as God, who had just begun.
One day at a time; one place to start;
To share a bounty of wisdom and wealth within our heart.
To create an image of mankind, Jesus would become His Son;
To walk the earth and try to teach almost everyone.
A chosen living being at that time;
Unfortunately, many saw this as a crime.
To take away the gift of light that was given for free;
Only to acknowledge the King Jesus came to be.
As it is written, it has been done.
Now the Father and the Son are really only One.
Joseph Esposito © 10/26/2017

I was given another message the day I wrote that poem and titled it "The Father and The Son." My belief in the Father and the Son come from the scriptures in the Holy Bible, which speak of Jesus, the King of Kings. To get to the Father you must go through Jesus Christ the Son first. You cannot love God the Father without loving Jesus the Son. If you do not believe in Jesus, then you do not really believe in God.

Jesus, while still fully God, became fully man, through the Virgin Birth. Angels appeared to Mary and Joseph to tell them what would happen, and Mary became pregnant with Jesus, the Son of God.

Acts 2:17: And it shall come to pass in the last days, says God, That I will pour out of My Spirit on all flesh; Your sons and your daughters shall prophesy, Your young men shall see visions, Your old men shall dream dreams.

Acts 7:51: You stiff-necked and uncircumcised in heart and ears! You always resist the Holy Spirit; as your fathers did, so do you.

Acts 17:30: Truly, these times of ignorance God overlooked, but now commands all men everywhere to repent[.]

Acts 17:31: [B]ecause He has appointed a day on which He will judge the world in righteousness by the Man whom He has ordained. He has given assurance of this to all by raising Him from the dead.

Acts 19:2: [H]e said to them, "Did you receive the Holy Spirit when you believed?" So they said to him, "We have no so much as heard whether there is a Holy Spirit."

I have said many times that going to church is a preference that we choose. God does not live in a church.

Acts 17:24: God, who made the world and everything in it, since He is Lord of heaven and earth, does not dwell in temples made with hands.

Acts 26:8: Why should it be thought incredible by you that God raises the dead?

Acts 26:18: To open their eyes, in order to turn them from darkness to light, and from the power of Satan to God, that they may receive forgiveness of sins and an inheritance among those who are sanctified by faith in Me.

Acts 28:27: For the hearts of this people have grown dull. Their ears are hard of hearing, And their eyes they have closed, Lest they should see with their eyes and hear with their ears, Lest they should understand with their hearts and turn, So that I should heal them.

Romans 2:7: [E]ternal life to those who by patient continuance in doing good seek for glory, honor, and immortality[.]

Romans 8:14: For as many as are led by the Spirit of God, these are sons of God.

Romans 8:28: And we know that all things work together for good to those who love God, to those who are the called according to His purpose.

Romans 12:2: And do not be conformed to this world, but be transformed by the renewing of your mind, that you may prove what is that good and acceptable and perfect will of God.

Romans 12:21: Do not be overcome by evil, but overcome evil with good.

Romans 13:1: Let every soul be subject to the governing authorities. For there is no authority except from God, and the authorities that exist are appointed by God.

Romans 13:8: Owe no one anything except to love one another, for he who loves another has fulfilled the law.

Romans 13:11: And do this, knowing the time, that now it is high time to awake out of sleep; for now our salvation is nearer than when we first believed.

Romans 14:11: For it is written: "As I live, says the LORD, Every knee shall bow to Me, And every tongue shall confess to God."

Romans 15:13: Now may the God of hope fill you with all joy and peace in believing, that you may abound in hope by the power of the Holy Spirit.

Romans 16:20: And the God of peace will crush Satan under your feet shortly. The grace of our Lord Jesus Christ be with you. Amen.

Joseph Esposito

Almighty Father

Oh, Almighty Father up above,
Thank You for showing and giving me so much of Your love.
You are always teaching me how to learn to grow.
Now I ask You Almighty Father, teach me how to show.
I have learned so much that You have chosen me to know.
You have been giving me Your words to teach;
There are so many lost souls we need to reach.
I am always ready from the moment I awaken;
For You, my Almighty Father,
have replaced all that was once taken.
Each morning when I rise to Your touch,
Oh, I thank You Almighty Father, for You have given me so much.
Joseph Esposito © 1/15/2018

Hope of deliverance from the darkness that surrounds us. My proof is already written in the Holy Bible. Only by diligently reading it many times over can anyone understand the scriptures, including those above that I chose to include in this chapter. Even these I did not select on my own. The Holy Spirit guided me to the ones that should be included.

When I started writing this chapter, I only had a title. The rest came from reading the Bible and letting the inspiration come.

Sometimes, with all that I have been through, I am amazed that I can even spell anymore. It was one thing that I did excel at in school, however. I had a great teacher who made it fun and I learned to enjoy it. I even won a fifth-grade spelling bee.

Everything inside our bodies can be repaired with the proper care and time. Our bodies were designed to heal themselves. Our spirit is no different. Prayer time, meditation time, and down time in a quiet place will rejuvenate the mind, body and soul. Modern medicine cannot cure everything. Sometimes the cure, like some cancer treatments, can be worse than the disease.

God created our world, including all of the plants and herbs and roots. In many cases we have forgotten about those, and their healing properties. We go straight to the chemicals and the radiation. It is our time to wake up.

Chapter Twenty

TIME AFTER TIME

Job 40:14: Then I will also confess to you That your own right hand can save you.

Time after time and day after day we tell ourselves little lies. We believe that a change is going to come into our lives. But we fail each day because of the lie we told ourselves the day before. It might have been:

I will start to lose weight tomorrow; or
I will become a better parent starting tomorrow; or
As soon as I have the time I will do (fill in the blank); or
It will be easier on New Year's Day to start fresh; or
I will start going to church after I go to confession; or
I do not have the money to change anything now; or
I am waiting for you to start and then I will begin too; or
After this week passes I will start over; or
When my back pain subsides, then I can (fill in the blank); or
(10) You get the picture!

Excuses and reasons are stories we tell ourselves time after time to justify inaction. We want to make changes, but we continually block ourselves and remain stuck for another week, month, year or decade; even permanently.

As the words play over in our mind and we continue to stand in front of our dressing mirrors, we realize that our clothes do not fit as well as they should any more. One more daily reminder – our reflections telling us that we are liars. Time after time we stop on the way home from work at our favorite bar to have a beer, glass of wine, or some other drink. We say we will be home in no time at all. This may work for some. Many cannot walk away that easily.

When we forget how to help ourselves because our daily habits and rituals have become permanent fixtures, our self-denial acts out in our minds. We do not believe we are strong enough to break away from our own demise – from the choices we choose to make once again. Everything applies to numbers in all that we are doing. Be it one or a thousand times, just like they say in the Alcoholics Anonymous or Narcotics Anonymous meetings: "one is too many and a thousand is not enough."

Our eyes tell our story. When we cannot look at ourselves anymore, it is time for massive change. Our secret fires keep burning over and over again. When our eyes have us blind and our bodies are trembling with fear and doubt, we know we are in trouble again because of the same lies we told ourselves yesterday and the day before. It may just be that perfect time to call out to a higher power; to let down our guard and repent.

Quitting is never a positive gesture unless we are quitting something that has held us down for too long or has been taking years off of our life. Then, the quitter becomes a winner in the first minute they choose to redirect the voice that has been cheating them out of their time. Help is everywhere. Every minute thereafter that we continue correcting and redirecting our steps, the word winner should play over and over again in our head.

We each have a borderline within us, something like the red line on our car's tachometer. Once we have redlined, we know something is going to blow because anything over that redline is the danger zone. If the night becomes our world, chances are we are playing fast and loose with self-control. Tomorrow can seem far away because of the hell we live in each night. The four walls we surround ourselves with do not have to become our prison anymore. Our hearts are still beating for good reason. Until we loosen the cobwebs in our minds that have us trapped like a fly in a spider's web, we may reside in our own self-imposed hell.

Love may only be a four-letter word. Now combine it with two other four-letter words: "your" and "self." Combine them and you have a powerful two-word statement: love yourself. Peace of mind is only one thought away. No one need be perfect to love themselves. We are in competition with no one but ourselves. Breaking the code of silence within ourselves to raise our awareness will allow us to break free. If you think that there is nothing you can say or do, just let these two simple words – love yourself – come to your emotional rescue.

We cannot try anymore, we must do. We cannot lie anymore, we must become true. This is not a dream anymore. It is time to let go of the nightmares we continuously hang onto. Nothing from nothing leaves nothing. When we feel nothing, we must run from ourselves and shut the door that kept us prisoner. We may not see ourselves as others do. That will never be okay until we understand our circumstances and stop giving in to sin.

Maybe you do have a death wish. The pain that you feel is very real. But I am here to tell you that you do not really want to die with that kind of pain. You really do reap what you sow and if you have been reaping for the devil, then you will be sowing a bigger seed in the afterlife.

Galatians 6:8: For he who sows to his flesh will of the flesh reap corruption, but he who sows to the Spirit will of the Spirit reap everlasting life.

Clean up your mess and retain your dignity. We must not attempt to fulfill righteousness without prayer. God answers prayers promptly and unmistakably. We should learn through Jesus how to pray.

Seek God's glory in all things. It is our duty to pray for others. Jesus' thrice-uttered prayer of agony should teach us: (1) how much he suffered for us; (2) that it is not wrong to be exceedingly sorrowful; and (3) whatever we pray for, we should always submit our will to God's.

Everyone is searching for a hero. The greatest love of all is inside of you and between you and God. Find your hero. Step out of your own shadow and reveal yourself. Find your strength in love.

Revelation 1:3: Blessed is he who reads and those who hear the words of this prophecy, and keep those things which are written in it; for the time is near.

I believe that God reveals His deeper truths to the eye of faith. Those who come to the Bible in a devotional spirit, seeking to know more of God and His will regarding us, are the most blessed. Human knowledge must be understood to be loved, but divine knowledge must be loved to be understood.

Ephesians 5:14: Therefore He says: "Awake, you who sleep, Arise from the dead, And Christ will give you light."

Ephesians 6:11: Put on the whole armor of God, that you may be able to stand against the wiles of the devil.

Ephesians 6:12: For we do not wrestle against flesh and blood, but against principalities, against powers, against the rulers of the darkness of this age, against spiritual hosts of wickedness in the heavenly places.

Ephesians 6:21: But that you also may know my affairs and how I am doing, Tychicus, a beloved brother and faithful minister in the Lord, will make all things known to you;

Sometimes I wonder if Tychicus is my ghostwriter. The Bible is a living text. The truths in this book speak loud and clear. Everything in the universe, and your own universe, can and will change. But the truths in the Holy Bible never change.

Chapter Twenty-One

What Time Is It?

Deuteronomy 6:7: You shall teach them diligently to your children, and shall talk of them when you sit in your house, when you walk by the way, when you lie down, and when you rise up.

"What time is it?" someone may ask.

"What time would you like it to be?" you may respond, instead of just telling that person what time of day it actually is.

Time is only a number on the clock. Or is it? When we cannot find our way home, maybe we do not care anymore what time it is. Whether it is because we are wasted from drugs or alcohol abuse or just burned out from working endless long days, our mind is breaking inside of our head. We may just believe that we do not have the time anymore to do what is right. Are we using this as a reason, or just as another new excuse?

Maybe it is time to just move on and give up our haunting past. Maybe it is the right time to focus on what is real. Maybe we are just afraid of the numbers, like our weight or our age. Forget about what the date on the calendar says, or the time on the clock, or the number on the scale. Those are just reminders. Time is not on our side unless we know what we are doing with our time. Free yourself: financially, physically, mentally, spiritually. It is only too late when we stop trying. Time will only repeat a habit that cannot be broken. Something

Joseph Esposito

inside of us has died and we must rework our inner clock. Salvage the remains that lay deep under your skin. It is only too late when we are dead and buried. Until then, we can rise again. If you are reading this, it is definitely not too late. Life is all around us. Wake up. See it. Feel it. Figure out what time it really is. Time is unconditional and so is the timeless Holy Bible.

Unconditional

Unconditional love and support,
Too many of us forget and abort.
A childish game of give and take,
Your life is your own choice to make:
To live in regret or stay forever upset.
Because of your own selfish needs,
Out of control like a garden of weeds.
To continuously build a wall of hate,
One day you will see, just you wait.
To hold and carry a hidden anger,
You are on your way to becoming a stranger.
So many years have slipped past.
Time is starting to move very fast.
Maybe it's time to listen to your inner voice
And make a move to a better choice.
It is never too late to make it right.
Life is too short to always fight.
In your time of need, you may be left alone to bleed.
Life and love should always be unconditional.
Joseph Esposito © 7/10/2012

Broken Dreams

Broken values and broken dreams,
Nothing ever is what it seems.
Two steps forward and one step back,
You waste your whole life trying to get back on track.
Time is ticking fast as each day goes past.
You cannot turn back the clock.
You try to turn the key, but it will not unlock.
As another day fades away,
There is always hope if we pray.
Joseph Esposito © 1/24/2013

I often wondered why and where the words come from when I am instantly inspired because of a conversation or comment, or just from looking out the window of my ice cream truck and seeing children laughing and playing in the park on a particular day – a sight I have seen thousands of times before. What is special about that time, that conversation, that comment?

I remember the very first poem I ever wrote. I was inside my ice cream truck, waiting in the parking lot of Danbury High School, for the after-school programs to finish. I was thinking about my daughter Alishia and I started writing a poem titled, "I Thought You Would Like to Know." It flowed straight from my heart.

One of two things happen in this life: either we are a victim of our own circumstances or we are victorious because of our circumstances. The choice is really ours.

No-man's land may be the safest place to be, a place where we can find our own sanctuary. In the search for our destiny, with our burning desire to change the minds of the lost souls we encounter, no-man's land can leave us feeling that something is missing. So we continue the quest in our search for the final answer to our final questions. Remembering the pain that is still locked away, deep in our mind, where we thought it was safe. Changing our direction, walking away from those old memories, may take a little longer than we thought. Searching our souls may not happen if we are living in denial, depression, or solitude. All are dark places in our minds that will still block us from going where we really want to go.

The Past

Sometimes the past goes by so fast.
You may have some regret,
Something maybe hard to forget?
Life is a gamble, the road that you choose.
You do not know if you win or lose.
To live is to learn; to live is to earn.
I know it may sound funny,
But it's not always money
That makes you what you are.
Sometimes we stop and wonder how we got this far.
Joseph Esposito © 11/26/2010

Moving past our painful memories can cause us to remember the days that mean nothing anymore. They should no longer have any hold on our personal freedom. Let them go.

Slow and steady is a safe way for doing almost anything. Doing something is almost always better than doing nothing. We all have wants and needs, things to do and places to go. Sometimes we can be held against our will because of physical pain or severe illness. During these times, we have no choice but to slow down and possibly even stop until the pain subsides or the illness goes away. Our bodies are not like machinery. Sometimes we need a little more than a screw tightened, or a bolt replaced. We feel pain, but we cannot always see its source. Pain wears us down if it becomes chronic or severe. It can become a huge negative factor in our daily lives, impacting us mentally and emotionally, as well as physically.

We all have some sort of physical pain. Many of us live with pain daily. We speak of a pain "threshold." For some it is higher than others and we manage to live with seemingly more pain with fewer disruptive consequences. Physical pain thus becomes a personal problem, unique to each individual. Only we can relate to our own personal pain and how we handle it.

Pain is a remembrance that we are only human. Our bodies break down from time to time. We need to take care of them as best we can when we are able. Eating right, exercising. I will not claim it is easy. The old saying, "no pain, no gain" is definitely true. But to the extent you can, even if it is just walking every day, do not neglect your physical needs. Life is a physical journey as much as a mental and spiritual one. Physical strength is an asset worth having.

With God, everything is possible. This applies to everything we do: work, play, love, life. We constantly struggle with the direction we are taking with our lives. We have to live in the physical world. We have to make a living. But we were not created by God to make money. We were created for a spiritual purpose, to worship and honor Him with the lives we live. We are all connected on a spiritual level where money is not the currency. We have to make money to live, but we do not have to live for money. Just as the sun shines for everyone, we should all try to shine as brightly as we possibly can while living in this world.

Life has many levels of play. Walking and talking without direction, without purpose, can be quite useless. Have a purpose. Exercise, teach people about God. While living our daily lives we can get lost along our way. We try to fill our emptiness with material things that will mostly be forgotten, rather than sharing our talents with charitable organizations, enjoying the arts or music, learning a martial art or studying the Word of God.

Joseph Esposito

The world today watches, listens and communicates through electronic devices. Sit in any restaurant and watch a typical family today. Are they talking to one another, exchanging stories of each other's day? Or are they all looking at their devices, heads down, not paying any attention at all to one another?

When it seems impossible, remember that all things are possible with God. We do not have to go across the country or anywhere, for that matter. Let our mind go to Him. God knows our thoughts. He understands our needs and knows what is holding us back. Do not be afraid to reach out to the Holy Spirit and pray instead of wallowing in your shadow and shame. Do not blame God for your sins. Amen.

Eye of the Beholder

When you look at your life
as a whole picture of goodness and sadness;
As life has ups and downs;
When you look at your opposite other and wonder;
Where the years have gone because
time has a way of changing face;
And so many other things may be out of place;
If your heart is in the right place, your eyes will never deceive you.
Sometimes we have to with our heart and not our eyes.
Beauty will always be in the eye of the beholder.
But love will follow us as we get older.
Joseph Esposito © 2/21/2012

Let God become your shelter and forget about what time it is.

Chapter Twenty-Two

LIFETIME

Psalms 13:1: How long, O LORD? Will You forget me forever? How long will You hide Your face from me?

A lifetime may seem like a long time, but in a sense a lifetime is not a long time at all. By the time we have it all figured out, we may not have much time left to do the things we once only dreamed about. Once we know how to create time by rising early and devoting our time to work to our advantage, we will have mastered managing our time diligently and discretely. Many years must pass by before we even acknowledge the meaning of wasted time.

Time is essential, but because of human nature and human behavior, we always think that we have more time. Perhaps at twenty-one years of age, we think we have at least another sixty years to make up for wasted time. That could not be further from the truth. Fatal accidents happen every day. Disease is everywhere. No one knows what will happen tomorrow, or if there will even be a tomorrow.

When we are dreaming with a broken heart, waking up is the hardest part. We roll out of bed and for a moment we can hardly breathe. Our head hurts from the night before and maybe we are not even sure why because we blacked out. What will it take for us to understand that we have lost control? The bottle that we long for has no answers to any of our problems.

When we become aware that our world is crashing all around us in our lifetime – here and now – it is still true that we can find a better way. We are our world. We cannot go on pretending that we are all we need. Being strong is being free; being selfish is not.

When we are down and out, when there is no one left to call and taking another step alone will only make us fall, there is another choice we can make to save our life. We must first be able to give before we can receive. When our lifetime becomes our new life-wise, we own our admittance to resolve the black hole we have fallen into. The light at the end of the black tunnel will be waiting for us there.

Like the fire on the mountain when God delivered the Ten Commandments to Moses, we must rewrite our own commandments and shake off our last demons that have been suffocating us.

My personal prayer request:

"God grant me the strength, courage and energy to follow the dreams of my heart. God help me to stay strong on my feet. Give me the stamina to help me move and run fast and never walk away in defeat; to always believe in You and myself. God grant me the power to never hurt with intention but allow me to protect my loved ones and anybody that needs my strength through Your supervision. God please allow me to expand my comprehension and give me the ability to learn quickly and correctly as I may have lost some time from my past. But I have never lost faith or my love for You. I know in my heart that You are the greatest teacher. You are the most powerful of all creation. God grant my family, friends and others Your safety net and protection from disease. Help them in the many ways that only You may know. I ask You for so much, I know, but only You are capable of such a grand request. All I can ask is for Your best. Thank You my Beloved Father in Heaven. Amen."

For You

They say if there is a will, there is a way.
Do not put off till tomorrow what you can do today.
Choose your path of life with a clear mind.
Listen with your heart and don't get left behind.
Use the tools that God has given you.
Always smile and be friendly, even if you don't want to.
Don't be anyone's fool; always keep your cool.
Always believe in God and yourself; don't give in to sin.
Trouble is just around the corner, you will see.
Don't bother with those strangers, just let them be.
Hold your head up high; don't be ashamed to cry.
Learn to forgive and forget; don't live life in regret.
Time is yours to take; it's only up to you what you make.
It's always better to give than receive;
trust in your heart and believe.
You have everything to gain and nothing to lose.
Always dress well and don't forget to polish your shoes.
Don't be afraid to live and share your dreams.
Don't overplay or live beyond your means.
The voice that is heard more is always soft spoken.
Keep fighting to not let your dreams become broken.
Stay strong in your heart and mind.
Remember not to listen like you are blind.
Always give one hundred percent and nothing less.
Always remember to just be yourself and be your best.
Joseph Esposito © 1/25/2013
(This poem is dedicated to my wonderful grandson Cayden Joseph)

Joseph Esposito

If I

If I should break before I fall,
What would it take to hear my call?
If I should cry before I awake,
How will I know if it is not fake?
What joy or sorrow will tomorrow bring,
If I cannot come to you listening?
If I knew before what I know now;
If I can be better, stronger somehow;
If I can live this life with you again;
If I am still here, just say the word.
Amen.
Joseph Esposito © 1/27/2015

Life is a journey filled with happiness and many sorrows in between heaven and earth. Between the seen and unseen, revelations that exist in the minds of many. Desires that many dream about here on earth, if not acted upon have no meaning. Life is a gift from heaven and a dream to live here on earth. A combination of good and great expectations. Live with no expectations or without acceptance of an abstinence to resolve a personal debt within your own being.

Allow yourself to be exposed from the inside out. Our information can become a great value, not only for ourselves, but for many people who do not know who we are. Who we are is not important. What we learn and share with others is. Sorting through the higher intelligence that has been received is critical information to share amongst the lesser minds.

Gain momentum with words to teach in rooms filled with people that need our knowledge. Great things happen when least expected. Learn to keep a relaxed mind. Not anticipating results will be one of our best weapons. High expectations, mixed with anticipation, can hurt our effectiveness. Learning to control our mind is like having money in the bank.

Our minds have many rooms. Some of these rooms have more space than others. A musician can learn to play many different types of instruments. Some are similar, and some are very different, but a skilled musician can compartmentalize the skills and draw on them as needed for perfection on each instrument. Someone fluent in multiple languages has a comparable skill, as does a martial artist skilled across multiple disciplines. By changing the channel or compartment in our mind, we can be at our best in any situation.

Mindfulness and mindlessness are complete opposites. Mindfulness is when a person is very thoughtful and respectful toward another person. Mindlessness, on the other hand, is where proper manners are disregarded, and bad habits replace self-discipline and integrity. The choice is always ours. First, choose to make a change. Decide to move forward or remain in solitary confinement. Live in the moment that is now and remove yourself from where you have been hiding. Dare to live.

Timing is everything and there will be no better time than the present time. Tomorrow will begin. Will you? Can you? The answer has always been yes. A new day is waiting. The opportunities are endless with the right mindset. Free your mind and free yourself.

The Bible tells us that with God all things are possible, that angels watch out for us, and that we never know when we might be entertaining angels. I want to relate an experience I had one night that makes it easy for me to believe all of the above.

Dr. Ronaldo, my wife Elisabet and I were headed to a distant city in Brazil in January 2018. We had already driven three hours from Ituiutaba to Uberaba where Dr. Ronaldo's mother and brother live. After a quick stop at their home, we got back on the road headed to Ribeiro Preto for a graduation party for Dr. Ronaldo's daughter. She had just graduated from medical school, following in her father's footsteps. We were driving a not quite two-month-old 2018 Ford Focus, fully loaded with everything electronically controlled. Something malfunctioned and the car shut off on the open highway.

Dr. Ronaldo made a phone call to his brother, Pastor Flavio. Unrelated to that call, however, a huge flatbed tow truck pulled up behind us within approximately ten minutes without any of us having called for it. Ten minutes later, we were all safe and sound riding in the backset of this huge truck and the car was on the flatbed being towed to a presumably safe location. We felt pretty fortunate. There are many thieves in Brazil who look for broken down cars. At gunpoint they do what they want to the unlucky people standing at the side of the road and steal or strip the car. If it had been two hours later, it would have been dark, and we would have been at the mercy of the nocturnal rattlesnakes that live in the cornfields that surround the road where we broke down.

God sent an angel of a man at the perfect time.

As we drove back to Uberaba with the tow truck driver, he suddenly pulled over and started backing up to a ramp that is only for the cars to enter onto the highway. We all instantly became alarmed. There is so much corruption in Brazil and if this driver was corrupt, he could have made us, and our car, disappear. No one would have ever known.

But he was not corrupt. God had sent an angel of a man and he had seen a car that had turned over. It was stuck between two mounds of dirt with water just below the car. The driver of the car was very fortunate: if the car had gone into the water, he might have drowned or died from a poisonous snake bite. Instead, he had just enough room to get out the driver's side window of the car without a scratch and our tow truck angel saw him and stopped.

Coincidence? Dumb luck? Maybe. But I do not think so. I believe God always has a plan. Dr. Ronaldo is a very blessed man. He is a cardiologist who has been saving people's lives from heart disease for over forty years. His brother Pastor Flavio is also a blessed man. He has been a pastor for more than thirty years. Even if Pastor Flavio called a tow truck driver, it could not have arrived as fast as our driver arrived. I believe God sent that man. I believe this man was either doing God's good works, or he was an angel.

All in all, it was quite an experience. It was ten p.m. when Dr. Ronaldo's wife Elaine came to pick us up and we once again got on the road to complete our journey to Ribeiro Preto, but the detour was definitely not a waste of time.

Chapter Twenty-Three

Time to Imagine More Energy

John 15:5: I am the vine, you are the branches. He who abides in Me, and I in him, bears much fruit; for without Me you can do nothing.

TIME: To Imagine More Energy. That is how I like to define time.

Life Without Hopes and Dreams

Life without hopes and dreams would be
a life without reason.
A life without reason would lead to a path of destruction;
that would lead to darkness and despair;
that would restrict your limits to live in this crazy world we live in.
Hope and dreams means to live in a positive mindset.
To live in darkness and despair is to live in a negative,
thoughtless life that would end in death.
Joseph Esposito © 12/17/2010

Joseph Esposito

Sad World

It's a sad world we live in today.
Many people have lost their way.
There are still so many left hopeless, living out there.
Where will they go? What will they do?
So many of us don't care. What if it was you?
As we live every day in this temporary home,
One day we will be on our way, where we will never be alone.
To reach out to a higher power,
One should not wait until their final hour.
We need to prepare from the inside now.
If you read in the scriptures, it will tell you how.
Accepting the fact that no one lives forever,
Some of us may not care and just say, "Whatever."
There is a God waiting up above.
This God is our Maker; He is compassion and love.
Those who still do not believe,
Will suffer the most on the day they cannot receive.
Life is full of hopes and dreams and choices.
God has many ways to get through to you.
If you listen, you just may hear His voices.
Joseph Esposito © 2/2/2013

Age

Age is only a number and how you may feel.
The higher the number is no big deal.
Age is in the eye of the beholder.
Not to worry, because you are getting older.
Life is a game of numbers and what you do.
Time is all we have in this life. It is only up to you

How you feel and react to your age.
We are only human; we are not meant to live in a cage.
Be happy that you are still here.
So many of us vanish each and every year.
Do your best to try not to get stressed.
Play your game of life well;
It's only a matter of time that will tell.
Joseph Esposito © 2/1/2013

Blessings

How many blessings can you count on your fingers and toes?
God has given you so many; that's something only God knows.
Blessings may come in different shapes and colors.
Blessings from within, or maybe through others;
Blessings from above, or blessings through love;
Blessings that start a new day;
Learning to live life in a different way.
Blessings through another person's eyes;
Blessings come from near and far, or maybe from a shooting star.
Blessings can come in so many ways,
Blessings just watching how your new baby plays.
Joseph Esposito © 2/1/2013

Perfect

Nothing is perfect in this world, or so it seems.
Perfect I am not; only in my dreams.
A lack of confidence or self-esteem,
Can disassemble my mind into extremes.
What may not seem perfect to some,

Joseph Esposito

Still I have to believe in something or someone.
Too many wrongs can never make one right.
I give it my all and do my best to sleep at night.
Humans were not created to be perfect.
Don't be discouraged and don't be deceived;
I am only as good as I believe.
Joseph Esposito © 2/4/2013

Special to Me

Special to me is something you will always be.
These feelings inside I just cannot hide.
You are like a brand-new toy,
So much better because you are a beautiful boy.
It is something I had never thought too much about,
I remember the day she gave me the news –
I did not need to shout.
You see, she is special to me, my one and only.
So that makes you special to me; now nobody is lonely.
There are just so many things to say.
You bring new hope and joy each and every day.
You are so much more than one could hope for.
She is so blessed that God opened for her a new door.
In this life we live we have so much more to share and give.
As you start getting older knowing who you are,
Your talents and possibilities will be unlimited.
She is the same, born with so much creativity.
You are both very special to me, and life's longevity.
I can only thank God that she is still here.
I hope and pray that together your light will shine brighter each and every year.
Joseph Esposito © 7/10/2012
(This poem is dedicated to Alishia and Cayden.)

Without You

Without you I would never know
so many new faces every time I go.
Your friends come from near and far,
They love you just the same no matter where you are.
You have a special gift of light that you shine,
I am very lucky to say that you are mine.
Even with good days and bad, I never like to see you sad.
You have a heart that is true;
my life would not be the same without you.
You have taught me to live life in a better way,
For this I am thankful each and every day.
I know I don't say it enough, without you my life would be tough.
You will always have a place in my heart.
With or without you, I took a vow: "Until death do us part."
Joseph Esposito © 2/3/2013
(I dedicate this Poem to my wonderful wife Elisabet.)

I often wondered why so many words that have come into my mind became poetic stories. I know the answer to my question these days. All the times I was able to write these types of poems, either from being sad or from something that caused me pain, I was able to take that sadness or pain and turn it into a joyful and powerful poem. For this I often thank God for using the broken times in my life to gently and kindly put healing words in my troubled mind. God is a warrior in so many ways. The word warrior ways that He has blessed me with seem to be limitless.

I chose to include some of my poems in this chapter to close this book with positive choice words just as they were given to me. Everything I have been able to write is personal to me. I speak with authenticity and honesty, just as it has been spoken to me.

Joseph Esposito

Every time I have gone to Brazil has been special and an amazing experience, but the last time, in early 2018, was a time of monumental personal growth for me. I feel that I grew mentally and spiritually. I became much more aware of living in the moments that have been given to me.

In this life that we all live, storms will come. Everything that happens to us happens for a reason. It is what we do with our time and with what happens to us during these storms that matters. We can react negatively and make the storms so much worse. Or we can accept that there is something for us to learn by going through them, and they will not seem as catastrophic in the moment or in the aftermath. Hurricanes and earthquakes happen all over the world. It is often during these tough times that people are brought closer together and learn to work together again to heal their communities. In the end, they are often stronger than they were before.

In the aftermath of some tragic events, it is not possible to get back to where we were before they occurred. Quite simply, things have changed. We must move on. Everything will be handled accordingly, either by man or by God. The biggest mistake one can make in life is to think or assume that God does not exist. Not believing in God is a choice. It is a choice to go on doing exactly as we have always done before, living our life without God. The wrong choice. Love yourself. Love God too. Better yet, love Him first.

Don't Know What You've Got Till It's Gone

This old saying is so true:
to give up what you already have and
leave your life up to chance;
to look for a new romance;
To take another turn in a different direction,
 just because you are looking for perfection.

You must look in the mirror and
ask your reflection what is really in your heart;
and do you dare yourself to make a new start?
To give up all that you've created for selfish needs,
or give it another try until you succeed?
Once you throw your love away,
you may never find true love another day;
look in your heart to find another way.
To keep what is already yours is a better choice.
In time you will know true love and then you can rejoice.
Life is short. Love is forever.
Joseph Esposito © 12/19/2010

Blessed Be God Forever

Why do some people wait so long
To not believe in something so powerful and strong?
Something you cannot see or touch;
Words that were written that say so much.
What is it that is so hard to understand?
What will it take for Jesus to walk this land?
With so many things in this life to be thankful for,
Always wishing and hoping for something more.
Only the people that struggle to not believe,
They are confused about a religion they cannot receive.
The day will come sooner than we think.
On this day everything you had ever hoped for
can easily be gone in a blink.
Blessed be God forever.
Joseph Esposito © 2/7/2013

Joseph Esposito

Love

Love is for sharing; life is for sharing;
love is for caring; life is for caring.
Time is for caring; time is for sharing.
It is essential to give equal amounts of love and time.
But allow yourself to share time with yourself
as well in an equal part.
Because if we are not happy, no one will be happy.
So let's all eat, drink and be merry and live and love;
share and care to make the right changes,
choices and adjustments to not cause stress in our daily lives.
It's only our time that matters,
but most important how we choose to use it.
We are going to be here for a while,
the least we can do is live, laugh, love
and always share our smile.
When we wear our smile,
 God will share His smile.
Amen!
Joseph Esposito © 6/21/2012

Because I Can

Because I can do what comes to mind,
I have a mind of a different kind.
Because I can feel the unseen power,
I can recreate by the hour.
Because I can listen to what must be heard,
I can hang on to your every word.
Because I can do what is right,
some may like to argue and fight.

Because I can find power when I am weak,
I can listen when the Lord chooses to speak.
Because I can revel in the moment,
 I can stay straight and never get bent.
Joseph Esposito © 1/21/2016

Chapter Twenty-Four

The Power of God in Time

ethany ... We should recognize God's power; God hears prayers at all times.

The Power of God- verse 1

When you feel His power in your final hour,
It may then be too late to believe;
only the faithful shall receive.
Another chance to do what is right;
Jesus only needs the faithful for this fight.
Countries that continue to build walls of hate,
 Jesus will put on a show and demonstrate.
These countries and people will war no more.
The change will come as a surprise;
only the faithful will witness through their eyes.
Joseph Esposito © 2/7/2013

The Power of God- verse 2

The power of God is all around in churches and places;
 people who believe – it is seen on their faces.

The Almighty Father, the King of Kings,
lives high above His Angels' wings.
There are many here that speak God's word,
His Kingdom, His Power is clearly heard.
People who live to disobey, their lives will never be okay.
Their sins and their lies will only cause pain;
for this reason, their lives will have no gain.
Joseph Esposito © 2/7/2013

The Power of God- verse 3

Our God Almighty is the greatest Pastor;
He is not only our Creator, He is our Master.
As Satan reaches for Heaven's gate,
God's Angels and Saints tell Satan he has to wait.
Satan is one of a kind, a deviant master of disguise;
it may be only something God can recognize.
Satan should know by now he can never win.
Satan was an angel himself but committed the ultimate sin.
The power of God Satan knows too well;
as now Satan lives below in his kingdom called hell.
Joseph Esposito © 2/7/2013

The Power of God- verse 4

The power of God can be connected in so many ways.
God's Kingdom is Heaven, where He stays.
His laws were written in a book many years ago.
It's called the Bible, something you should already know.
It's hard to understand, but God is the ruler of this land.
We are His people of many different kinds,
many different languages, and many different minds.
Joseph Esposito © 2/7/2013

The Power of God- verse 5

The power of God will have no end.
God can be always and forever your friend.
Even after you die just as Jesus,
you may get a second try.
Life as we live now, in the afterlife,
Jesus will show us how.
You can think what you will,
God has a higher power still.
You have more to gain and nothing to lose,
but you must choose.
Joseph Esposito © 2/7/2013

The Power of God- verse 6

There is no time in Heaven as time stands still.
There are no worries or pain so do what you will.
To get to Heaven you must believe and do some good;
 raise and teach your children and family to believe as you should.
Heaven is a place for reconnecting people that died.
Life can be everlasting in Heaven for many who have cried.
Joseph Esposito © 2/8/2013

The Power of God- verse 7

As God created man,
God also created a plan.
A long time ago,
there was not too much to know.
Many years have now passed;
everything is done very fast.

Joseph Esposito

God is still in control,
waiting for a time to make a change.
As most countries like to have
more power and exchange.
Fighting has never been the
answer to this resolve;
It only causes more friction when
another country is dissolved.
Joseph Esposito © 2/8/2013

The Power of God- verse 8

In this world in which we live there
can only be one God that can give.
One should never forget, today may be your last.
Every day we pray to our Father
to thank Him for our past.
As we live in the present moment of time,
There is so much to be grateful for in our mind.
If you live to see tomorrow, do not forget to pray.
Just be thankful for the gift of living
to see another day.
Joseph Esposito © 2/17/2013

The Power of God- verse 9

Jesus is the Son of God,
this we should know.
God only created One
 so many years ago.
Jesus was once in the flesh
but died on the cross.

For the people that knew Him,
it was a terrible loss.
God had this planned,
 long before Jesus' birth, as only God can.
The Lord our God finished His work,
even before it began.
For some it may be hard to
believe and understand.
God creates miracles
where nobody else can.
Just like God,
Jesus lives not yet to be seen,
In a place called Heaven;
not earth but somewhere in between.
Joseph Esposito © 2/17/2013

The Power of God- verse 10

God our Father and Jesus
now can work together as One.
The power of God will come back
through His Son.
It is only a matter of time
 when Jesus will reappear.
This will be another test of
God's faith somewhere.
It is very important not to make
the same mistake.
Jesus died once;
now this time His life you cannot take.
Just as you believe in your children,
believe in Jesus too.
If you have no belief or faith,

Joseph Esposito

When Jesus comes, what will you do?
Joseph Esposito © 2/18/2013

The Power of God- verse 11

The war that continues in Israel has to end.
They will have to prepare for the Savior God will send.
Two thousand years have already passed.
The grounds of Israel have been trashed.
The once land of the Man who would become King.
When Jesus comes, with Him freedom He will bring.
Joseph Esposito © 3/4/2013

The Power of God- verse 12

With each day that goes by it is a day closer. Why?
Jesus has waited a very long time for this day.
A new revelation from His maker to go on display.
Many problems to solve; many people to heal.
A time to give back from the ugly and the evil that steal.
Joseph Esposito © 3/4/2013

God Is

God is the final judge;
He sits on a throne that no human can budge.
God's world is your choice;
first understand and listen to our King's voice.
God is a marvel and a wonder,
waiting for us all who live down under.
God is amazing and true; He is searching,
hoping to find you.

It is your choice to be found;
let Him in and He will be your ground.
God will never ask for more than your best;
He already knows the worst,
so let Him have the rest.
A life devoted to God will not always be
the easiest you have known;
But He does promise that you will
never, ever, be alone.
He chose you because
he knew you were already lost;
The price for you was paid by Him --
paid in His blood at the Cross.
Joseph Esposito © 1/31/2016 (modified 3/18/2018)

God has filled our minds and hearts with a garden of beauty, but it is up to us to show our true colors and flavors. We have an unlimited amount of power and energy just waiting to be exposed. Love God, love yourself and then love others.

ABOUT THE AUTHOR

Joseph Esposito is the author of three books,
Time Escapes, Seeds of Life and *On a Mission of Nutrition.*

Joseph Esposito

Addison Grace

I am overjoyed by the gift of life
that has been given once again.
Addison Grace,
a granddaughter who will grow
to be much more than a friend.
With the many blessings received to date,
I never thought there could be one more.
Cayden now has
a new baby sister to look after and care for.
God is never late to create or recreate.
Addison Grace has an amazing, beautiful face,
Blue eyes and a perfect smile,
as she is very curious
looking around all the while.
Addison Grace will grow to be strong and wise
just like her brother.
Cayden and Addison are both truly blessed
to have Alishia, my daughter, as their mother.
As I pour my heart into words-
as they flow-
I know God's true intent is the gift of life,
but still too many of us may never know.
Amazing Grace shines through the blue eyes
of Addison Grace

Joseph Esposito (c) 7/29/2018